DATE DUE

PRINTED IN U.S.A.

DIRECTING THE ACTION

•

Acting and Directing in the Contemporary Theatre

•

CHARLES MAROWITZ

APPLAUSE

THEATRE & CINEMA BOOKS

Directing the Action
Acting and Directing in the Contemporary Theatre

Copyright © 1986 by Charles Marowitz

A cloth edition of the book was originally published under the
title *Prospero's Staff* by Indiana University Press.

Library of Congress Cataloging-in-Publication Data
Marowitz, Charles.
  [Prospero's staff]
  Directing the action: acting and directing in the
    contemporary theatre / by Charles Marowitz
  p. cm. — (The Applause acting series)
  Previously published as: Prospero's staff.
  Includes bibliographical references.
  ISBN 978-1-55783-072-2 : $16.99
  1. Theatre — Production and direction. 2. Acting. I. Title.
    II. Series.
PN2053.M36 1986b
792'.0233 — dc20
91-27849
CIP

British Library Cataloging-in-Publication Data
A catalog record for this book is available from the
British Library

Applause Theatre & Cinema Books
33 Plymouth Street, Suite 302
Montclair, NJ 07042
Phone: (973) 337-5034
Fax: (973) 337-5227
Email: info@applausepub.com
Internet: www.applausepub.com

Applause books are available through
your local bookstore, or you may
order at www.applausepub.com or
call Music Dispatch at 800-637-2852

Sales & Distribution
NORTH AMERICA:
  Hal Leonard Corp.
  7777 West Bluemound Road
  P.O. Box 13819
  Milwaukee, WI 53213
  Phone: (414) 774-3630
  Fax: (414) 774-3259
  Email: halinfo@halleonard.com
  Internet: www.halleonard.com

EUROPE:
  Roundhouse Publishing Ltd.
  Millstone, Limers Lane
  Northam, North Devon
  EX 39 2RG
  Phone: 01237-474474
  Fax: 01237-474774
  roundhouse.group@ukgateway.net

FOR JANE ALLSOP,

JANE APPLEBAUM,

JANE WINDSOR,

&

JANE MAROWITZ

CONTENTS

FOREWORD
by Peter Brook

Why does a director direct? To help an actor act? Or to make a play play? Both? Neither? Give this simple sentence to a linguistic philosopher, and at once the seeming simplicity vanishes: What does direct mean, what are its direct, its indirect meanings? Why was a director originally in England called a producer, why a "putter on stage" in France, a "stage manager" in opera? Are directing, producing, putting and managing different ways of describing the same thing? It is not surprising that Charles Marowitz feels the need to write a book to throw light on this confusion.

The confusion goes further. Actors and authors periodically claim that directors are quite unnecessary, and I am forced to admit that one of the most powerful emotions a director can experience is one of intense shame when he observes the distortion of plays and the destruction of actors that take place regularly in the name of directing. In fact, this authoritative act is a two-edged blade with which every director can make or mar whatever he touches.

I began working in the theatre not with any particular love for it. It seemed to me a dreary and dying predecessor of the cinema. It was because at twenty no one would give me a film to direct that I turned with appalling condescension to the task of producing a play in the only tiny theatre that would have me.

In the weeks before the first rehearsal, I carefully prepared my script as for a movie. The play began with a dialogue between two soldiers. I decided that one of them should be discovered tying his boots, and that the fifth line would be enhanced if in the middle of it the shoelace snapped. The first morning, I wasn't at all sure how a professional rehearsal starts, but the actors clearly indicated that we should sit down and begin with a reading. I at once told the actor playing the first soldier to put on his shoes as he read. Somewhat surprised, he complied, leaning forward, his script awkwardly balanced on his knee. In the middle of the fifth line, I told him the lace should now come apart. He nodded and went on reading. "No," I stopped him. "Do it." "What? Now?" He was amazed, but I was amazed at his amazement. "Of course. Now." "But this is a first reading. . . ." All my latent fears of not being obeyed came to the surface; this act smelled of sabotage, of authority disputed. I insisted; he angrily complied. At lunchtime, the lady who ran the theatre gently took me aside. "That's not the way to work with actors. . . ."

It was a revelation. I had imagined that actors, as in a film, were hired to do at once what the director wanted. After my first reaction of injured pride had subsided, I began to see that the theatre was a quite different affair.

That did not mean that I gave up the idea of using a stage to make moving pictures. Every production I did was built on images that I wanted to see in flesh and blood, but I realized that the actor could vastly enrich this canvas if he was given his freedom. One day a West End manager said to me: "The actors tell me they are quite lost in this scene. It's up to you to teach them what to do." I was disturbed and not too pleased. I was a picture maker and a show maker—an actor had his own job to do, and he was supposed to have been taught already. For this reason, I surrounded myself usually with very experienced and famous actors who could be trusted to do their own special cuisine in their own special way, and whose results could easily be blended into a coherent pattern.

However, ten years of satisfying work led to a point at the end of the fifties when nothing was satisfying anymore and everything came into question. I wrote a piece called "Search for a Hunger," and another called "Oh, for Empty Seats!" in an avant-garde theatre magazine of which Charles Marowitz was an editor. Turning to films, I gave up theatre, to my mind indefinitely, but in fact for two years. Returning at the invitation of Peter Hall to join him and Michel St. Denis as codirectors of the Royal Shakespeare Theatre, I now knew my own vital need: to be able to explore the nature of theatre experience in laboratory conditions at the same time as I was working for a wide audience.

That brought Charles Marowitz and me together. I had long been interested in and impressed by Charles's sharp and pitiless analysis of all that was wrong with whatever he saw on the London stage, and I found that he also needed a framework to put his ideas into practice.

We formed together a little unit of actors that we rather grandly named the Theatre of Cruelty. We had no precise aim; we wanted to discover what an actor is, what a group means, what a play is made of, and what the human being, unaided, can express, emanate, and evoke in front of an audience. We worked in the dark, inventing all sorts of exercises as though we knew how, advancing in what was at the time virgin territory. We learned an enormous amount by trial and error.

It was a good partnership; Charles was an admirable collaborator, not only because of his intelligence and enthusiasm but also because of his infinite hypercritical capacity not to be impressed—essential for the health of any experimental work. Charles is never at a loss for words, but in the thousands of phrases that we exchanged over the months one in particular touched what had been gnawing at my subconscious. Charles was talking about an ideal group and defined it as "one in which the energy passes from one actor to another all through the performance, bringing about a constant flow of rich creativity." Yes. That was what was lacking in all the ensembles of good professional actors in the past. That is what we were looking for.

The different meanings of directing became clearer. A director can treat a play like a film and use all the elements of theatre, actors, designers, musicians, etc. as his servants, to communicate to the rest of the world what he has to say. In France and Germany, this approach is much admired, and it is called his "reading" of the play. I had come to realize that that is a sad and clumsy use of directing: it is more honorable if one wants to dominate totally one's means of expression to use a pen as a servant, or a brush. The obvious alternative is the director who makes himself the servant, becoming the coordinator of a group of actors, limiting himself to suggestions, criticisms, and encouragement. Such directors are good men, but like all well-meaning and tolerant liberals, their work can never go beyond a certain point.

I think one must split the word *direct* down the middle. Half of directing is, of course, being a director, which means taking charge, making decisions, saying yes and saying no, having the final say. The other half of directing is maintaining the right direction. Here, the director becomes guide; he's at the helm, he has to have studied the maps, and he has to know whether he's heading north or south. He searches all the time, but not haphazardly. He doesn't search for the sake of searching, but for a purpose: a man looking for gold may ask a thousand questions, but they all lead back to gold; a doctor looking for a vaccine may make endless and varied experiments, but always towards curing one disease and not another. If this sense of direction is there, everyone can play the part as fully and creatively as he is able. The director can listen to the others, yield to their suggestions, learn from them, radically modify and transform his own ideas; he can constantly change course; he can unexpectedly veer one way and another; yet the collective energies still serve a single aim. That enables the director to say yes and no and the others willingly to assent.

Where does this "sense of direction" come from, and how, in fact, does it differ from an imposed "directorial conception"?

A "directorial conception" is an image that precedes the first day's work, while a "sense of direction" crystallizes into an image at the very end of the process. The director needs only one conception, which he must find in life, not in art, which is a sense of what an act of theatre is doing in the world, why it is there. Obviously, that cannot come from an intellectual blueprint; too much committed theatre has sunk in the whirlpool of theory. The director may have to spend his life searching for the answer, his work feeding his life, his life feeding his work. But the fact is that acting is an act, that this act has action, that the place of this action is the performance, that the performance is in the world, and that everyone present is under the influence of what is performed.

The question is not so much "What's the event about?" It is always about something, and that is what pinpoints the director's responsibility. It leads him to choose one sort of material rather than another—not just for what it is, but because of its potential. It's the sense of the potential that then guides him to finding the space, the actors, the forms of expression, a potential that is there and yet unknown, latent, only capable of being discovered, rediscovered, and deepened by the active work of the team. Within this team, everyone has only one tool, his own subjectivity. Director or actor alike, however much he opens himself, he can't jump out of his skin. What he can do, however, is recognize that theatre work demands of actor and of director that he face several directions at the same time.

One must be faithful to oneself, always believing in what one does, yet faithful to the knowledge that the truth is always somewhere else. For that reason, one values the possibility of being with oneself and beyond oneself, and one sees how this in-and-out movement grows through interchange with others and is the basis of the stereoscopic vision of life that the theatre can bring.

I have just made a series of vast generalizations. In another context, I would regret that, as theatre work is all the time a matter of specifics: it is practical, concrete, or it's nothing at all. But as this is an introduction, Charles Marowitz can now take over. It is good to hear this voice speaking articulately and probingly from his own experience. Listen to him.

INTRODUCTION

The first professional production I ever directed, at about the age of sixteen, was a modern-dress version of *Doctor Faustus* in an old union hall called Labor Temple on the East Side of New York. I remember very little about that show except that I had managed to secure the services of a genteel English gentleman, much advanced in years, to essay the lead. Although he was somewhat short on passion and liked to deliver the most fiery and rhetorical speeches from a sitting position, he did bring a certain clarity to Marlowe's words that added dignity to the occasion. Unfortunately, the accents of the rest of the cast ranged from Brooklyn to Louisville, and so the overall diction of the piece left a lot to be desired.

What I remember more vividly than the production itself was the transference of certain notions I had privately conjured up onto second parties and the sense of power that conveyed. Everyone on the stage became a conduit for my own energy, an extension of my personal inventiveness. A director, my teen-aged sensibility seemed to be confiding to me, was a kind of God who made actors in his own image. He could infuse them with his intentions, shape them to his will, and in so doing, they could become his emissaries in the real world. Through them, he could create a multifaceted force of which he was the secret commander, and by adopting certain methods, it was possible to make a great noise in the world and still remain hidden. That was the first stage of the seduction that was to continue for the rest of my life.

Gradually, as I directed more and more plays, I became aware that there was a power even greater than the director's, and that was the collective power of the company, which, properly harnessed, was the most potent force the theatre could unleash. But to find the source of that power involved endless quests. There were no maps, no formulae, no short cuts. The only tools were intellect, instinct, and the cutting edge of the play. But no matter what the strategy, the underlying impulse and overriding aim of all these searches remained conquest.

Anyone who denies the power drive of the director, who talks about "expressing oneself" or "helping actors to find themselves" or "being involved in teamwork," is deluding himself. The director is a self-obsessed colonizer who wishes to materialize power through harnessing and shaping the powers of others. It is not a calling for shrinking violets or self-effacing nonentities—although it is sometimes a haven for both.

There are many parallels to the art of directing in Shakespeare's play *The Tempest*. Prospero is in many ways the most impressive director that ever was. Having "bedimm'd The noontide sun, call'd forth the mutinous winds, And twixt the green sea and the azured vault Set roaring war," he clearly has a weakness for spectacle. Like many authoritarian directors, he is crotchety, cantankerous, and a severe taskmaster—as he demonstrates with Ferdinand, whom he commands to pile up thousands of heavy logs. He is also something of a showoff, and not above trying to dazzle Ferdinand and Miranda with his skills: "For I must bestow upon the eyes of this young couple," he tells Ariel, "some vanity of mine art—it is my promise and they expect it from me." Whereupon he launches a most eye-catching pageant with a cast of deific superstars, including Iris, Ceres, and Juno, and a large supporting cast of nymphs, reapers, and assorted sprites.

But supernatural spectaculars aside, Prospero is also a rather sensible regisseur employing sound tenets of psychology. He imposes strenuous tasks on Ferdinand, an aristocratic young man not accustomed to manual labor, not out of cruelty but as a means of proving the young man's love for his daughter. And because Ferdinand's love is sincere, his "mean task," which should be "heavy" and "odious," transforms into pleasurable labor. When he is done, Prospero, like a wily director who has worked an actor hard for his own good, confesses that all of Ferdinand's "vexations" "were but my trials of thy love," and having passed the test, Ferdinand achieves a union that had it been more quickly won, might have yielded less happiness and proved less durable.

The severity with which Prospero imposes his task on Ferdinand conceals the end for which it is undertaken. Despite the brusqueness of his manner, his intention is sympathetic, and his method constructive. The same is true in regard to Ariel, that most spectacular of all stage managers.

When Prospero finds Ariel, confined for a dozen years within a cloven pine—a punishment inflicted upon him by the vindictive Sycorax, who ruled the island before his arrival—he releases him. True, he then makes him his slave, but Ariel's duties are always meted out on the understanding that he will one day be set free. So, as with Ferdinand, Prospero instills a profound motivation in his underling. Prospero's attitude to Ariel is stern, even overbearing, but he is also sympathetic. Again, like a director who knows that an actor must be rigorously exercised before he is given free rein over his character, he puts Ariel through his paces and, when the time is ripe, grants him his freedom.

In his efforts to improve and instruct his creatures, Prospero even attempts to refine the bestial Caliban—"making much of him" and teaching him "how to name the bigger light, and how the less, that burn by day and night"; in return for this instruction, he wins Caliban's love and persuades him to reveal "all the qualities of the isle." Eventually, Caliban's licentiousness and innately evil nature turn him into a despised slave, and yet, despite his disloyalty, Prospero finds it in his heart to forgive him. At the end, Caliban spurns drunkards and pretenders and gratefully returns to Prospero. Like an actor seduced by every kind of indulgence, Caliban ultimately accepts his director's authority as the best means for achieving "grace."

Prospero is the rightful Duke of Milan. He handed the administration of his worldly duties over to his brother Antonio, because he was more concerned with "the liberal arts" and intellectual pursuits. Antonio, seduced by the powers he had acquired, usurped his brother's authority and arranged for him to be removed from his position and, with his daughter, sent to his death on a "rotten carcass of a butt" in a wild and treacherous sea. But a benevolent Neapolitan, Gonzalo, provided clothes, food, and books for the banished duke, and through a stroke of good fortune, Prospero landed on this enchanted island, where, in exile, he became a different man.

The director, like Prospero, does not live in the hurly-burly world of trade and commerce. He, like Prospero, preferring books and study, inhabits his own enchanted island, where he develops his powers and gains a different perspective on the "real world": sees it objectively and without illusion. When he was Duke of Milan, i.e., in the midst of the day-to-day business of government, Prospero had no supernatural powers. Like his usurping brother, he was simply a duke—but one with no appetite for the office. When he arrives at his enchanted island with his books, his staff, and his meditations, he becomes Prospero—that is, an embodiment of the learning he has always craved.

At the end of the play, after he has revealed his true identity to his brother, and called for his "hat" and "rapier," the symbols of respectability and self-defense, he promises a full explanation. "At pick'd leisure, Which shall be shortly, singly I'll resolve you, Which to you shall seem probable, of every These happen'd accidents." A few speeches later, he again promises to reveal the significance of "particular accidents gone by Since I came to this isle," but in fact, he never delivers these explanations. Instead, his books "drown'd" and his magical staff broken and "buried certain fathoms in the earth," he returns to the mundane person he was before being ousted from Milan. His "charms overthrown," his strength now only that of a mortal man, he acknowledges himself "most faint." Once his worldly powers are restored, his supernatural powers disappear. The master director, abandoning his gifts, his ability to shape circumstance, asks to be accepted again as an ordinary member of the public. "As you from your crimes would pardon'd be . . ." [i.e., indulging in fantasy and pretense] Let your indulgence set me free."

The Tempest is not only about reconciliation and forgiveness, but about the relinquishment of power. For many, because this work is thought to be one of Shakespeare's last, the figure of Prospero abandoning his magical powers has come to represent the author bidding farewell to his profession. But for me it has always been more like a director forsaking his special, somewhat lofty, vantage point and joining the rest of the audience merely as a spectator: a process that happens at the conclusion of every rehearsal period, when, in a sense, the director abdicates in favor of that new authority—the public.

In fact, Prospero's staff, buried all those many fathoms in the earth "and deeper than did ever plummet sound," is regularly unearthed by directors of all ages, who, like Shakespeare's wily old wizard, muster bright and dark spirits into their service to create theatre. As with Prospero, it is done out of love or revenge, out of a desire to convert or enthrall, or simply to show off, and as in *The Tempest*, it reconciles the artist and his public. But it is, as Prospero calls it, "a rough magic," and one that ultimately must be abjured: that is, exchanged for that purer magic that occurs not among spirits or gods but in the company of men.

And yet, to create the transformations wrought by a director in collaboration with his fellow artists, it is to Prospero's staff that one must look. For without that "rough magic," there is no theatre. And without a Prospero, Ariel can never be freed, Caliban reformed, Ferdinand and Miranda united, or a troublesome state restored to order.

(L to R) Oberon, Puck and Titania in Marowitz adaptation of *Midsummer Night's Dream*. Odense Teater, Denmark.

Fairies holding Bottom while Titania exhorts them to revelry. Marowitz adaptation of *Midsummer Night's Dream*. Odense Teater. Denmark.

Alexis Kanner in the Marowitz *Hamlet* —co-directed by Marowitz and
Peter Brook at the Theatre of Cruelty Season at LAMDA, London.

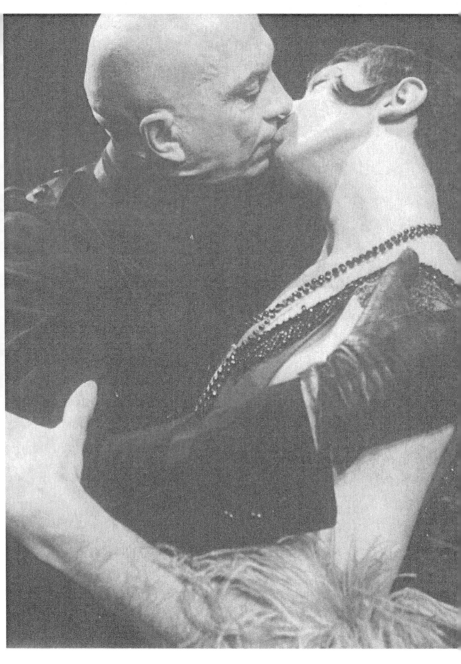

Oberon and Titania in Marowitz adaptation of
Midsummer Night's Dream. Odense Teater, Denmark.

Clive Merrison as Artaud in Charles Marowitz' *Artaud at Rodez* directed by the author at The Open Space Theatre, London.

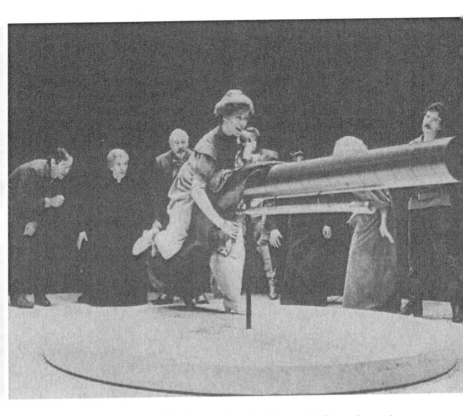

Jennie Agutter (Hedda) in Charles Marowitz' free adaptation of *Hedda* directed by Marowitz at The Round House. London.

Thelma Holt (center) as Katherine and Tim Hardy as Petruchio (above) in Marowitz free adaptation of Shakespeare's *The Shrew*. Directed by Marowitz for The Hot Theatre, The Hague, Holland.

DIRECTING
THE
ACTION

The Definition of Terms

If we date the emergence of the director from the late nineteenth century with the advent of people such as George II, the Duke of Saxe-Meiningen in Germany, Henry Irving in England, and Stanislavsky in Russia, we see that "direction" was essentially a form of discipline imposed, usually by one strong-minded individual, upon the sundry arts of the theatre. In imposing that discipline, the theory of unified production, vigorously espoused by Richard Wagner and later by Gordon Craig and Adolf Appia, comes about almost as a matter of course, and brings the authoritarian "regisseur" into being.

But the imposition of discipline from a firm central authority is not the same thing as insinuating personal interpretation. Firmly correlating all the working parts of a production is an activity closer to stage management than it is to direction. Unless the director brings a dimension of his own, namely, the expression of those ideas that constitute a personal viewpoint, we tend to deny him that distinction we have come to associate with modern directors.

Viewed this way, the Duke of Saxe-Meiningen (or was it his gifted stage manager Ludwig Chronegk?) was little more than a committee chairman. His mastery of crowds, his meticulous attention to detail, his obsession with costume accuracy—all of these are laudable goals, but they do not in themselves constitute "direction" as a distinctive creative force.

In Henry Irving's company, and particularly his period at the Lyceum Theatre, we had the same kind of imposed discipline, accuracy, and attention to detail in the hands of an inspired actor-manager. But whatever virtues we may ascribe to Irving the director, they were coincidental to his work as an actor working among other actors. Although he assimilated and, in some cases, actually improved upon the techniques of the Duke of Saxe-Meiningen, he was still functioning as an actor-manager, that is, a manager of actors and the fulcrum of a theatrical management. Although anyone who exercises taste on the construction of sets and costumes, the disposition of actors, and the expedition of stagecraft is *directing*, still we do not associate Irving with unique individualistic interpretations of the plays he produced, nor can he qualify as a director in our contemporary sense of the word.

With Andre Antoine and Victorien Sardou in France, Arnold Daly in New York, Constantin Stanislavsky in Russia, and Max Reinhardt in Germany, the director, armed with a viewpoint, a stylistic prerogative, and an aesthetic bias, gradually comes to the fore. Here too are disciplinarians, chairmen of committees, if you like, but also men who are refining the work of actors and insinuating an artistic purpose derived from a personal view of theatre. (Significantly, the two most influential forces of the twentieth century are amateurs: Antoine, a clerk at the Paris Gas Company, and Stanislavsky, an upper-middle-class dilettante who operated an amateur dramatic society.)

In the twenties and thirties in France, with men such as Jacques Coupeau, Charles Dullin, Gaston Baty, Louis Jouvet, and Jean-Louis Barrault, and in Russia with Nikolai Evreinov, Eugene Vakhtangov, and Vsevolod Meyerhold, we begin to see the first signs of another kind of director: men who leave their mark on material as much as they do on actors; directors who begin to reveal an attitude to new and established plays that is more pronounced than before. Sometimes, aggressively so.

The emergence of what we would call the modern director coincides not with his imposed authority on the physical elements of production, but with his intercession with a playwright's ideas. The autocrat-director controls his actors; the modern director appropriates to himself those intellectual ingredients usually reserved for the playwright—using the tangible instruments of the stage as a penmanship with which he alters or gives personal connotation to the text of writers both living and dead.

That is most visible in the works of Shakespeare and with directors such as Max Reinhardt, Vsevolod Meyerhold, Benno Besson, Georgio Strehler, Peter Stein, and Peter Brook, who begin to produce resonances in established works that surprise audiences who never imagined the plays dealt with themes they now seem to be about. So that, for instance, there comes a production of *King Lear* that charts the rise of the bourgeoisie and the gradual disintegration of feudalism, or another production that treats the play as an Oriental fable entirely detached from any historical milieu, or a version in which it is seen as a bleak, apocalyptic vision unfolding in an arid, Beckettian landscape from which God has been banished.

In these instances and in many others like them, what has changed is the philosophical framework in which the play was originally conceived; the "spirit" of the work is radically rerouted, even though the "letter" remains intact. In short, another "author" has appeared, and he is saying things that are different from, sometimes at conflict with, the meanings of the first author; and this interloper is, of course, the director.

In a later chapter, I deal more fully with the question of interpretative license, so I will not digress here. My point is that the shift that has taken place in the theatre over the past eighty-five years is one that has brought a different kind of director to the fore, and for good or ill, he is the modern director: a man who insists on reading his own thoughts into those traditionally associated with the author whose work he is communicating.

Often, he resembles the autocrat-director of old. He is a stern disciplinarian. His taste is evident in every department of the production. His mise-en-scène is a straitjacket on which he and he alone tightens all the buckles. But despite resemblances to the Duke of Saxe-Meiningen or Henry Irving, he is not merely a supreme coordinator or advocate of one acting style over another, but a multifaceted artist in his own right with all the prerogatives, personal idiosyncrasies, and unpredictability one associates with the ilk.

A director who does not proceed in this way, who chains himself to unwavering fidelity to the author and pursues his work in selfless devotion to the "meaning of the text," is unknowingly abdicating a director's responsibility. Since the only way to express an author's meaning is to filter it through the sensibility of those artists charged with communicating it, *fidelity* is really a high-sounding word for lack of imaginative output. The director who is committed to putting the play on the stage exactly as it is written is the equivalent of the cook who intends to make the omelette without cracking the eggs. The director is the master of the subtext as surely as the author is of the text, and his dominion includes every nuance and allusion transmitted in each moment of the performance.

Writing against the director's tendency to reconceive the moments of a play, Maynard Mack, the Shakespearian scholar, says:

> The most obvious result of sub-textualizing is that the director and (possibly) actor are encouraged to assume the same level of authority as the author. The sound notion that there is a life to which the words give life can with very little stretching be made to mean that the words the author set down are themselves simply a search for the true play, which the director must intuit in, through and under them. Once he has done so, the words become to a degree expendable.

That is the academic "dim view" of theatrical innovation put in the most succinct terms, and it hinges on the phrase "search for the true play." If the director is able to "intuit in, through and under" the words, that makes them not "expendable" but capable of infinite variety. The play the twentieth-century director "intuits" from the seventeenth-century masterpiece is as much "the true play" as the one performed in the author's lifetime. It is the passage of time and the accuracy of a director's perception that determine the "trueness" or "falseness" of a play.

In other words, creative process is what confirms or transforms a writer's meaning, and the director is, quite literally, the master of creative process. He is the man who is "making the play happen again" and, in so doing, demonstrating its ability to *mean* again and perhaps mean something else. For Maynard Mack and his ilk, the play is a "given," and as such, there is a tacit obligation to deliver its original intentions. For contemporary directors, it is an invitation to undergo process, and only when that is done can its "meaning" be understood; and because theatrical process is inextricable from contemporary sensibility, the play is either proved or disproved through the act of interpretation. When Artaud exclaimed, "No more masterpieces!" he not only meant that we must lose our myopic reverence for "classics," he also meant that the present, like a court of appeal, must confirm or deny the presumed greatness of a "masterwork."

The hard evidence for such an appeal is the director's view of the work as performed by his company and received by his public.

Often in such cases, it is the interpreter's vision that is rejected and the masterwork, in all its traditional greatness, that is confirmed. But just as often, it is the artist's metamorphosis of the masterwork that wins the day, and when that happens, it *is* the director and his actors "who assume the same level of authority as the author." To view that as some kind of usurpation of proprietary rights is to misunderstand the nature of dramatic art and its tendency endlessly to reappear in different shapes and forms.

"The poet dreams up a play," said French director Gaston Baty in 1928, writing about Shakespeare, "and puts down on paper whatever can be reduced to words. But words can only express part of his dream. What is left over does not exist in written form. The business of the director is to restore to the work of the poet whatever was lost on the way from the dream to the manuscript."

The essential perception in these words is that a text is incomplete until production provides the culminating existential factor. The specious idea is that a director "restores" what a poet has lost in that passage between conception and creation. Surely only the poet knows what has been lost en route, and it is gross presumption for any director to say he is complementing, as it were, what the poet had not the presence of mind to furnish himself. The error in Baty's reasoning is still to assume that a director is obliged to fulfill the poet's original conception rather than provide a conception of his own, prodded, goaded, and inspired by the writer's original work.

What the poet can never provide is the social and historical ambiance in which his work is being revived. As much as he may understand human nature and the complexities of the human soul, he cannot foresee the priorities and preoccupations of future generations. He cannot interpret what his original imagery means to a public educated by and saturated in media imagery, for example, or the social and political pressures of the late twentieth century. He cannot appreciate, for example, that the crunch of the axes in *The Cherry Orchard* has as much an environmental repercussion for modern audiences as it does a nostalgic, or that the taming of a shrew by an overbearing male chauvinist adventurer cannot be seen outside the perspective of the women's movement of the past thirty years. It is in areas such as these that the director mediates between the author's vision and the public's and, like someone blending two disparate images, tries to fuse them into one.

The special virtue of a classic is that it can mean again and again—above and beyond what it originally meant. It is a compliment to its endless resourcefulness, its ability constantly to recreate itself like the chameleon that it is.

The modern director, then, is not simply a person who imposes order upon artistic subordinates in order to express a writer's meaning, but someone who challenges the assumptions of a work of art and uses mise-en-scène actively to pit his or her beliefs against those of the play. Without that confrontation, that sense of challenge, true direction cannot take place, for unless the author's work is engaged on an intellectual level equal to its own, the play is merely transplanted from one medium to another. A play that finds a physical corollary on the stage is not a play realized in another art form but one merely transferred from a passive to an active state. A performance that is not suffused with new dynamics proceeding from other temperaments and other viewpoints contradicts the essence of the word *perform*—which is "to carry on to the finish," to "accomplish," to fulfill the cycle of creativity begun by the author.

There are directors, and we know them well, whose greatest talent is their ability to induce artists to make distinctive personal contributions to the work at hand. They inspire actors to give their best, designers to operate at their most imaginative levels, and technicians to function at peak efficiency. A director may be capable of all these things and still be a rotten director. The coordinating and organizational skills of a director are basic to the calling—just as a painter must be able to differentiate between colors and comprehend light and shade. But these are easily learned technical requirements, not indices of creative potential.

An efficient director with "a wonderful way with people" is still negligible without the intellectual dimension to combat the work with his own creativity and to temper its assumptions with the heat of his own sensibility. Too often we talk of directors and mean the "shepherd of actors" or the "maker of schedules" or "the selector of colors." Too infrequently do we recognize that the central function of the man is to rethink and recreate the materials with which he works. The director who does not engage the animate and inanimate materials at his disposal and transmute them into an image of himself, is merely going through the motions. Some other title must be found for him. Call him a coordinator, a controller, a foreman, or a traffic cop, but do not confuse him with an artist of the theatre.

2

Director cum Playwright

There is no one more suspect than a director turned writer. He is like the crusty old bordello madam deciding to go on the game to show the girls how it should be done. Harley Granville-Barker, Tyrone Guthrie, Peter Brook, and Roger Planchon have all tried to step over the divide—none with outstanding results. And yet, Molière directed the plays he wrote; so did Noel Coward, and, according to certain scholars, so did Shakespeare. Brecht was perhaps the supreme example of the writer-director. Today Dario Fo successfully combines both functions. Harold Pinter does it occasionally with his own plays, more frequently with others; so does David Hare. The passage from writer to director, it would seem, is much more acceptable than the other way around.

If one were an actor, the transition would be taken to be the most natural thing in the world. John Whiting, John Arden, Arnold Wesker, Joe Orton, John Osborne, Alan Ayckbourn, and Michael Cristofer all started as actors and painlessly made the transition to playwright. But when directors sidle into that arena, it almost always is viewed as a transgression.

I understand this reluctance to accept the director as playwright. It is derived to some extent from the belief that a director is himself an artist at one remove, often a man who couldn't make it as an actor and therefore decided to withdraw from the heat of that particular kitchen—although anyone who has ever acted and also tried to direct will tell you that the difference in temperature is between a steam kettle and a blast furnace.

As far back as I remember, I have been writing—and in my

earliest, crudest exercises, writing dialogue. I specifically do not say "plays," because if a protracted period in the professional theatre teaches you anything, it is that the creation of a play, a *real* play and not a recycling of ingredients foraged out of an accumulation of available material, is even rarer than an original performance. So I say advisedly that I was a "writer of dialogues" rather than of plays, and I remained a writer of dialogues for most of the time I worked in the London theatre. Sometimes I applied my writing abilities to the plays I was directing—almost always when the author was dead, and occasionally when he was alive (often producing the result that he wished he *were* dead).

On those occasions when dead authors were not readily available, I have worked with live ones—John Arden, Joe Orton, Saul Bellow, Sam Shepard, Trevor Griffiths, Murray Schisgal, Peter Barnes, Arnold Wesker, etc. The collaborations were tense or calm, successful or unsuccessful, but always I operated as a writer—for a director exercising his critical temperament on evolving material *is* writing, even if he never puts down a single word. The impulse to cut, to change, to transpose, or to expand belongs to the craft of writing. It is born out of the needs of the written material before that material becomes palpable by being put into the hands of actors.

But I do not contend, therefore, that I was a playwright—or even a playwright's collaborator. I was a director performing the traditional functions of the director, which happen to include acts of literary emendation and, sometimes, creation. The director working with a playwright on a new work *must* be a writer if he is to have any validity as a director; and a writer, if he is worth his salt as a writer, accepts the director in that "literary" role. The director's literary impact is unavoidable.

Most writers fear change, and the engagement of the director is like the approach of the abortionist to a mother determined to have her baby. The tenacity of a writer's opinion on a particular question of production bears a direct relation to the consistency of his vision; and when a writer says resolutely that it *must be this way*, a director takes his life in his hands to say that it should be otherwise.

On the other hand, a writer whose talent is cast in clay rather than marble is the first to appreciate that a different idea born from his own text can sometimes be superior to his original idea, even when it contradicts it. That is not the author going back on his own word, but recognizing the fact that once that word is made flesh, it becomes another thing. A line of dialogue framed in an odd space, preceded by a pause and followed by an unexpected gesture, is no longer the line of dialogue as conceived by the author. It has become a strand in an existential process and is subject to new and different exigencies. An author who insists on the integrity of his original line in the face of all the new dynamics that now surround it is harking back to an earlier phase of development in the creative process: a phase when he and he alone was the arbiter of dramatic effect.

What as a director I learned very early on, and which for some authors is heresy, is that there comes a point in any play where language no longer serves a purpose—when, in a sense, things have gone too far for "words," and they must either be used sparingly or chucked altogether. In a good play, language engenders a network of associations in the audience's mind, so that a new language formed from action, rhythm, sound, and image takes over. To revert to the language that brought us to this new point of departure is retrograde. The precise value of language in the theatre is that it mounts progressively to those dramatic peaks where it becomes expendable— where some other power, a power generated by actors and action, begins to speak more eloquently to the audience. The author only cranks the propeller of the drama; it is the actors in the flying machine of the production that make the drama soar.

One of my most satisfying collaborations with a playwright was with Trevor Griffiths, author of *The Party, Comedians, and Sam Sam*, his earliest play, which I directed at the Open Space. What made it so was the fact that in all our discussions, Griffiths regarded the work objectively—that is, as a piece of material that, now freed from its chrysalis, fluttered in its own right.

He talked practically about what changes might conceivably make an inert scene come alive—without automatically assuming the scene already *was* alive simply because he had written it. He recognized that the engagement of actors different from the types originally conceived necessitated changes in the balance of a scene; that, for instance, material originally created for a sensual woman could not work the same way if the actress who had been cast was drier and more reserved; that different values could be found to take the place of those originally intended, and still the needs of the play could be served. During runthroughs, he was able to acknowledge that the rhythm of a scene halted not because of actor inadequacy but because something in the writing caused it to stick. Rather than insist that the actors should work harder to "get it right," he revised the trouble spot to remove the obstacle. His good sense persuaded him that "obstacles" were as much in the writing as they were in the acting, and even if they weren't, revision might still help to smooth the way.

Too often, the playwright believes that the root problem must be either in the actors or in the director's inability to get from them what the play requires. So long as problem-solving is attempted without testing the validity of the script, conflicts and resistances must arise. Griffiths, perhaps because he had done a lot of directing himself, tacitly acknowledged the fact that the rehearsal period was concerned with those problems thrown up by the fusion of writing and acting. He recognized that when these two vital elements were compounded, they produced an entirely new factor greater than the sum of each. That may sound like a simple deduction, but it is one that many playwrights find difficult to accept.

When I worked with Arnold Wesker on the script of *One More Ride on the Merry-Go-Round* (a comedy that at this writing has not yet been produced), I encountered a subtle mixture of compliance and resistance. The validity of certain criticisms was conceded, in general, but when they proceeded to deletions, large portions of the original script were defended on the basis of "texture." The Textural Argument (and it is so widespread that it deserves its proper noun) consists of a writer resisting cuts on the grounds that the material contains "living tissue" that, if removed, would weaken the overall consistency or texture of the play.

The validity of this argument is unchallengeable. It is possible to remove texture from a work in such a way that it loses precisely that quality that gives it distinction. (Imagine, for instance, the deletion of many of the epigrams from *The Importance of Being Ernest* on the grounds that they do not further the plot. The criticism sounds utterly legitimate. The epigrams are *not* needed to further the plot. However, the genius of the play depends upon the plot being not *furthered* but *retarded* by the ingenuity and sparkle of Wilde's wit, and so, by removing such "expendables," one virtually cuts the heart out of the work.)

The removal of material that contains texture does not mean *all* texture is lost. In a consistent work of art, texture permeates every part of the whole, so that even as one loses it in one place, it is retained everywhere else. (For example, deleting some of the epigrams from *Importance* would not destroy the epigrammatic feel of the overall work, as that is part of its essential tonality and *unexcisable* no matter what one cuts.) The removal of a cyst, a boil, or a tumor from the human body also involves the loss of texture, but the organism is often the better for the excision.

The Textural Argument is often a pretext for a writer overly defensive about losing any of his original work. So is the Structural Argument, which goes: "You can't cut that scene because it is an integral part of the overall structure." The great thing about the dynamics of play production is that structure is not rigid but malleable. You can alter sequences, rearrange incident, put the end of a play at the beginning and the beginning at the end, and still achieve its general intentions. "Texture" is not sacrosanct, and neither is "structure"—and often the preliminary work on the script involves deletions or alterations in precisely these areas.

The greater point about structure is that rehearsals tend to delineate a play's *existential* structure, which is more organic, and therefore more effective, than the one first evolved by the playwright without reference to living factors such as performers, design, playing time, and what happens to language when it coalesces with action. Structure, like everything else in the theatre, is a living thing and should never be thought of as "a given" or a fait accompli. There is virtually nothing that cannot be renegotiated in the rehearsal process.

Peter Barnes, with whom I worked on several plays, including the initial preparation of *The Ruling Class*, was a great stickler for structural fidelity and construed any attempt to shorten his work as a threat to its structure. Of course, if you cut twenty minutes out of a play, you must, of necessity, alter its structure, but if by making such a deletion you compress the action and remove unnecessary repetitions, you have restructured to advantage. *Structure* in the playwright's mouth is often a euphemism for resistance to cuts.

Writers as acute as Trevor Griffiths and Peter Barnes can be of invaluable assistance in rehearsals, acting as a kind of Geiger counter detecting false notes and wrong turnings. Others can be deadly in their subversion.

When I was directing the first performances of Murray Schisgal's

The Tiger and *The Typists*, the author used to lumber around the back of the auditorium, miserably rolling his head and biting his lip. The actors, needless to say, were disconcerted by the palpability of his pain, and I subsequently banned him from rehearsals—a decision he took to be unjustifiably high-handed. I had to consider on the one hand the composure of actors trying desperately to muster creative results, and on the other the overt agony of a writer who could not conceal his discomfiture over their efforts. Even if his agonies were entirely justified (and many of them were), that still created an atmosphere that militated against work.

Joe Orton, having been an actor himself and trained at the Royal Academy of Dramatic Art, was an exemplary writer in rehearsal. Whatever bothered him became the subject of long, discursive discussions after hours, but he always recognized the fact that during rehearsals, what the actors were attempting to do had to be zealously protected.

His conception of *Loot*, which I directed in London after it was abandoned in an earlier tryout, was curiously Chekhovian. Perhaps as an overreaction to the earlier production, which was heavy with horseplay and leaden with gratuitous jokes, he wished this production to be utterly sober and straightforward. When I was approached with the project aware of its calamitous reception in the provinces, I asked to see the very first version of the play before performers such as Kenneth Williams, Duncan Macrae, and Geraldine McEwan had interpolated their own inventions. That script, the pristine original, had all of Orton's subtle and sardonic humor resplendently intact, and it was that which I opted to direct.

But *Loot* was a black comedy with preposterous, almost Wildean flights of fancy—not a brooding Russian study of strained family relations. For Orton, the deliberate creation of comic moments inspired by the play's comic score was always considered an intrusion. Having observed the unchallengeable truism that real comedy must grow out of truthful behavior, and the wildest implausibilities must be plausible to the characters perpetrating them, he wished the rule to be applied with a vengeance. Had that been done, it would have turned the comedy into bathos and the Wildean capers into Strindbergian turgidities.

Here, what was at stake was degree, for there was no quarrel about the principle. But in the theatre, degree is everything. Too much verisimilitude in a comedy can just tip the balance between what is "straight" and what is "comic"—just as too much artifice can. Ultimately, one is dependent on the collective taste of the director and his company, and it is that, hopefully, which strikes the happy medium between pointing a joke and allowing it to sink without a trace.

Curiously, a reverse tactic was required in the production of Philip Magdalaney's *Section Nine*, which I staged for the Royal Shakespeare Company at the Aldwych Theatre. All my directorial energy went into eliminating the comic effusions of actors who felt that the way to inhabit a farce was with trousers down and noses painted red. The cast was a buoyant group of talented performers who wallowed in the pleasures of a play that wasn't a heavy European thinkpiece or a Shakespearian classic—their normal fare for several previous seasons. My popularity diminished rapidly as one rehearsal after another was spent repressing their high spirits and deleting their gallumphing improvisations. I knew the pitfall here was yielding to the brash, often sophomoric instincts of actors who were hell-bent for excess. Sometimes a director must be a divining rod encouraging the heavens to empty buckets onto the stage; sometimes, a finger resolutely plugged into a dike.

Many of the aforementioned instances are the predictable ups and downs of the writer's and director's passage through the troubled waters of rehearsals. What really rocks the boat is when a director suggests an alternative plotline or a different conception of character—when, in fact, he assumes those prerogatives that are traditionally associated with the playwright. Here, many of the purists will contend, the director is exceeding his limits.

Perhaps the most illustrious case of directorial initiative is Elia Kazan's 1955 production of *Cat on a Hot Tin Roof*, where the director requested and received an entirely different third act from the one originally devised by the playwright. Although Tennessee Williams obliged Kazan, he included his own version in the published copy of the text. It would be distracting and irrelevant to enter here into a discussion as to which ending is "better." What is more significant is that Williams, an established and celebrated playwright, respected his director's alternative vision sufficiently to supply the requested change. Williams's views on the director-playwright relationship are relevant to the issue under consideration:

> If you don't want a director's influence on your play, there are two ways to avoid it, and neither is good. One way is to arrive at an absolutely final draft of your play before you let your director see it! The other

way is to select a director who is content to put your play on the stage precisely as you conceived it with no ideas of his own. I said neither is a good way, and I mean it.

Not every playwright is as compliant as Tennessee Williams, but then not every director is as astute as Elia Kazan. Referring to Kazan's influence on the finished production, Williams writes: "The reception of the playing-script has more than justified, in my opinion, the adjustments made to that influence." But perhaps even more telling is Williams's admission: "I wanted Kazan to direct the play, and though these suggestions were not made in the form of an ultimatum, I was fearful I would lose his interest if I didn't re-examine the script from his point of view."

Certainly, there are occasions when a writer offers concessions in order to maintain the interest of a director he believes is going to benefit his play, but more important, it seems to me, is the acknowledgment that a play can be changed for the better as a result of taking account of "the director's point of view."

Williams's experience with Kazan is not unique. Once a director and writer begin to work intimately on the development of a piece of material, it is a little like two men huddled over the same canvas. Although the author provided the original painting, the director, in the act of collaboration, acquires a proprietary interest in the work. He comes to know its composition and color scheme as well as the author, and it then becomes the most natural thing in the world for him to proffer suggestions as to how the writer's characters might weave through the scenes, even taking certain detours never considered by the playwright.

Over the years, the rights of authorship have become the most treasured of all the artist's rights. "Right of authorship": the phrase itself rings in the ear like *Droit de Seigneur*; it implies total ownership and control, and, over many years of concessions bitterly won by dramatists, these rights have been enshrined in writers' contracts. It is hazardous to appear to undermine such achievements; however, the act of collaboration on a new work, as any writer will admit, is one in which the creation itself becomes an entity as separate from the writer as it is from the director. In the act of assembling, plotting, and refining the elements, a mutuality of interests is created that binds the director and writer into a new relationship, vis-à-vis the material. The director's vantage point, mingled as it is with the writer's, creates a new perspective on the work, and with this perspective, both director and writer can get a bead on the nature, structure, and texture of the material in a way the writer working alone cannot.

Of course, there are demarcation lines, but they cannot be set by contracts or union regulations. The sweat engendered by highly intensive joint efforts tends to smudge them.

When I was directing the premiere of Sam Shepard's *Tooth of Crime* in London, I found myself involved in a genuine territorial dispute. At the end of the first act of Shepard's play, he had written a long, descending speech for the character of Hoss, a fading rock hero who was soon to be superseded by Crow, a dynamic rock upstart. I felt that the ending dissipated the energy of the act and contained no imperative or "hook" into the next act.

Retaining the downward spiral of Hoss's speech, I added a tail-piece in which an incessant rock crescendo (played by the attendant rock group) grows steadily behind the immobilized figure of Hoss while simultaneously, in the background, a spotlight picks up the shadowy figure of Crow, whose myth had been regularly promulgated throughout the first act. At the final moment, as the light fades on Hoss, it comes up brilliantly on the sinister figure of Crow, resplendent in leather and studs—materialized for the first time. As the musical crescendo reaches its climax, the lights fade on the static figure, and we are into the intermission.

Shepard, who calumniated against what he called "outside" effects, was furious with the atmospheric change, the substitution of a charged climax for a dying fall. Clearly, that was neither what he intended nor what he had written. What these moments did supply was the director's need to create an act curtain that mobilized interest in the next act, for, having been introduced to this compulsive and challenging figure, the audience became eager to find out what kind of confrontation would ensue between the clapped-out champion, Hoss, and the newly arrived challenger, Crow.

In this case, the needs of the production outweighed, in my view, the shape of the original composition. Of course, whether such a change was justified was, and remains, a moot point. A downbeat ending may be as dramatically effective as a charged climax, but what is to be done when a director opts for *sforzando* where a writer has indicated *rallentando*? When the needs of the mise-en-scène collide directly with the author's needs? What happens, of course, is that all the political factors that swirl behind productions are immediately brought into play.

In this instance, the director of the play was also the artistic director of the theatre and had the full weight of management on his side, and so he carried the day. Had exactly the same difference of opinion arisen five years later, when Shepard's reputation was unassailable, and in a commercial situation where the director was more vulnerable, no doubt the *writer* would have carried the day. It would be comforting to believe that carefully assessed artistic considerations determine the outcome of interpretative disputes, but naive not to recognize that they almost always are decided by the arbitrary dicta of theatre politics.

At this writing, I am involved in a collaboration with Donald Freed, whose play *The White Crow* is being readied for production at the Los Angeles Actors' Theatre. The play is based, to a certain extent, on the actual interrogation of Adolf Eichmann after he was kidnapped and brought to Israel to stand trial for "crimes against humanity." When I was sent the first draft of the play, a loosely structured, underplotted reworking of the original interviews, my first instinct was to decline the offer on the grounds that the play was just too messy and unfocused to succeed.

But apart from its flaws, I had also had to acknowledge a gut reaction to its subject matter and what the author was trying to say through this material. Underlying the bald interview structure of the play was a more imaginative framework (based loosely on Dostoyevsky's *The Grand Inquisitor*) that used the Eichmann story as a way of exploring the moral dilemma of all Jewry in seeking "a guilty party" for the Holocaust—a quest that is in many ways futile, and certainly one that cannot be satisfied by the indictment of one man. What I responded to then was not the script itself but the presumption of greater significance in the material and the themes it was treating. After talks with the author, I overcame my initial reservations and agreed to direct the play on the condition that it was reworked.

The "reworking" has involved the inclusion of a third character, new additions to the conclusions of acts one and two, the incorporation of new material written by the director from selected documentary sources and subsequently integrated into the script, and half a dozen bits of new business that have altered the emphasis of several scenes throughout the play. In the case of every suggestion, I was obliged to justify the addition or emendation in terms of the original work, and in every case but one, my suggestions were accepted. The present version of the script—final only insomuch as it is the very last before rehearsals begin and the actors insinuate their influence—is a considerably different specimen from the draft originally submitted to me. In terms of actual playing time, I would estimate that at least one-third of the new work is attributable to my intercessions.

I do not broach this argument to imply any claims to authorship. On the contrary, I openly declare that Mr. Freed is the true and "onlie begetter" of *The White Crow*. But in fulfilling my director's function in the project, I have been obliged to "write changes" into the play. Whether he wished it or not, Mr. Freed has entered into a writer's collaboration with his director—and, hopefully, to his play's advantage.

Some time ago, a minicontroversy raged in the guilds about a director's royalty rights in regard to those plays where he actually contributes to the script—i.e., creates bits of dialogue or adds to the action and movement of a play in such a way as to influence its final, printed outcome. I believe it is both greed and misunderstanding that prompt directors to claim such rights. For whatever inventions a director may bring to a playwright's work, they would never have come about without the play as their inspiration—and as the playwright is the beneficiary of the actors' interpretation or the designer's conception, so is he the beneficiary of the director's inventions. The director's surrogate writing, or writing through osmosis, or writing by suggestion, or whatever one wants to call it, *belongs* to the writer as surely as the foliage belongs to the tree.

But no matter how strong the modern writer's claim to ownership (and as I have indicated, I think it is very strong), there is no denying the fact that in the case of certain classics, the imaginative creation of mise-en-scène is more pertinent than the play that gave it birth. I am thinking of productions such as Meyerhold's *Inspector General* or Orson Welles's *Julius Caesar* or Grotowsky's *Doctor Faustus*, where the creation of the production overmasters the text that inspired it.

Can one simply say of such works that they are outstanding productions of accepted texts? That beggars the description of all we know about Meyerhold's Gogol or Grotowsky's Marlowe. Here, a director, using the fine broad scrawl of his own imagination, has imposed imagery on an established classic in such a way that his own ideas predominate. And if we accept the notion that a director is the "author of the production," we also have to accept the fact that sometimes that "authorship" overwhelms the work of the original writer. Why else would we speak of Brook's *Dream* or Strehler's *Servant of Two Masters* or Planchon's *Tartuffe*?

Stanislavsky, by his own admission, served Chekhov, and Chekhov was the author not only of the plays but also of the productions. The wellsprings of psychological truth that Stanislavsky unearthed from the text were planted there by the author. Meyerhold, however, transformed Gogol, reconstituted Dumas, and thoroughly remolded Molière, and in searching out the taproots of those theatrical experiences, one is led back to the director and not the author.

The idea that a director, by reconceptualizing a work of art, can create an independent entity is, for most people, an impossible leap of the mind. Yet these same people have no difficulty in accepting that *Fratricide Punished* or *The Spanish Tragedy* is entirely different from *Hamlet*, or that George Whetsone's *Promos and Cassandra* is far removed from *Measure for Measure*—despite the fact that plot and characters from the former works inhabit and condition the later ones. A writer, it would seem, can extrapolate from given sources, but by no stretch of literary protocol can a director build a new artifact on the substructure of an extant play.

The theatre is full of "established practices" but has no rules, and so the director's relationship to a writer can be mild, as when a copyreader offers bits of punctuation or a changed word here and there to a star journalist, to sweeping, as when a film tycoon orders the total overhaul of a scriptwriter's first draft. Alan Schneider prided himself on the fact that his fidelity to an author was unwavering. For him, the director was the proverbial midwife and, as such, was charged with the safe delivery of the playwright's baby. Jed Harris, on the other hand, would freely rewrite an author's work and take immense liberties with character, construction, and plot. Stanislavsky, despite touches that drove Chekhov mad (a weakness for proliferating sound effects and a tendency towards gloom where the author intended gaiety), was a staunch believer in directorial obedience to the playwright's wishes. Meyerhold, as we have said, radically imposed directorial patterns on authors both living and dead.

Clearly, one cannot make a brief for gross distortion as a theatrical way of life, but neither can one piously intone the homily that the author should be "allowed to speak for himself." The only way the author can do that is to hire a hall and, taking all the roles himself, read his script to the assembled spectators. I am sure that even the most vigorous opponents of directorial initiative would flee the tedium of such a performance. When Shakespeare is "allowed to speak for himself," he invariably reveals a dullness of utterance that belies everything we have come to expect from this inspired writer. When, however, a creative director speaks *through* him, we experience his genius in ways we never suspected from our cloistered reading of the works.

A great play is only a sounding board for a great interpretation—which is just another way of saying that in the theatre, the resourcefulness of a writer is indissolubly linked to the perceptions of his interpreters and that one cannot possibly prosper without the other.

3

Masks and Faces:
The Casting Process

We often speak of an actor's "range." What do we mean by it?

A singer has a verifiable range—a compass of notes over so many octaves—but we don't measure an actor in such strict terms. When we refer to an actor's range, we are usually considering qualities such as the depth of his feelings, the stamp of his personality, the cast of his temperament, the pitch of his voice, the cut of his physique, the lilt of his accent, and other, less verifiable factors such as whether he is "strong" or "weak," "rough" or "smooth," "nice" or "nasty." The actor's social self—an extension of his inner self— is the vital factor in determining his suitability for any role, and the director, in assessing it, makes a judgment about the actor that is as much moral and philosophic as it is artistic. As a result of those assessments, some actors are banished to an irredeemable nether-world, and others are raised to the skies. As much as he may avoid the implication, when he is casting, the director is playing God.

The actor finds it virtually impossible to accept such judgments. He accepts them from no one else, so why should he accept them from a director? To be "judgmental" in our age is considered a negative trait, and yet, here is a man—or a group of men—declaring for all to hear that someone is not tender enough, not heroic enough, not spiritual enough, not tall enough, not handsome enough to play this or that role.

Of course, at the same time the director is playing God, the actor is making equally sweeping judgments about him. He may consider the director to be obtuse, banal, proceeding from stereotypical attitudes, unable to see beyond a polished or unpolished surface—a victim of hackneyed thought and petrified attitudes. What can he know of the actor's hidden depths, his ability to transform, to reveal colors never glimpsed in audition speeches or hurried readings of partial scenes? In other words, the actor rails against the stigmata of typecasting and vaunts his individuality as a defense against the system's remorseless categorical thinking.

In one sense, the actor can never escape being cast to type, for, physical considerations to one side, his character, like everyone else's, exists within given parameters. Why should it be commonplace for everyone else to be designated as nice, nasty, sympathetic, aggressive, feminine, macho, low-keyed, hot-tempered, congenial, or incorrigible, and for the actor to escape such labels? An actor may *well* be able to play a variety of types different from himself, but before considering that aptitude, he must recognize that there is a basic self by which he is known to the world, and it is not impertinent to ask that the constituents of his own character be taken into account before considering his ability to simulate others.

A casting director of my acquaintance believes that if an actor is talented he can play anything; that his talent, chameleonlike, can be transformed at will, and that the true distinguishing mark of an actor is precisely the exercise of such versatility. That is, at the same time, rubbish and incontrovertibly true. Any actor *can* be assigned to play any role and, technically, *can* play it, but if by "suitably cast" we imply a correspondence of traits and proclivities on the part of the actor in relation to his character, then limitations immediately present themselves. Being *well* cast means keeping those limitations to a minimum, and being *badly* cast means neglecting to take them sufficiently into consideration.

Let us put to one side obvious physical correlatives—height, shape, color, nationality, etc.—and accept that many of these can be ignored and brilliant casting still obtain. (We know, for instance, that one can sometimes create a startling effect by choosing a fat man where traditionally, a thin man is expected—or a black man in a part historically considered to be the province of a white man—or a female in a role intended for a male, etc., etc.) Let us put these exceptional choices to one side and consider instead those quintessential qualities that we look for in actors because we discern them in characters.

The essential factor in casting is recognizing the root quality of the actor: the quality that remains discernibly present after a variety of arbitrary characteristics have been imposed; the quality that, because it is indigenous, can never fail to surface, to some extent, in the final result. To recognize this root quality, the director must see beyond the prevailing impression created by past performances, beyond the stereotype implicit not only in the audience's perception of the actor but in the actor's conception of himself.

In London, there was an actor whose rough exterior and sharp features always inclined him to "heavies" but who, at base, possessed a sensitive, even tender, temperament. When, through a lucky accident, he was cast in a lyrical, poetical role, everyone was flabbergasted at his success. For years, he had been cast at face value—so much so that he himself had come to believe that he was a rough-hewn individual best suited for thick-skinned characters.

When Elia Kazan cast Marlon Brando as Stanley Kowalski in Tennessee Williams's *Streetcar Named Desire*, Harold Clurman was astonished. "When I first heard that Brando was to do the part," wrote Clurman, "I thought he had been miscast. For I had known Brando, whom I had previously directed in a play by Maxwell Anderson [i.e., *Truckline Cafe*] as an innately delicate, thoughtful and intellectually eager young man"—the same "delicacy," "thoughtfulness," and "intellectual eagerness" that Brando had displayed earlier in his portrayal of Marchbanks the poet in Shaw's *Candida*. And yet, there was no contradiction in the fact that Brando could also play the rugged Kowalski. Indeed, it was the actor's innate delicate qualities that gave that more primitive character his underlying sensitivity.

Kazan's audacity notwithstanding, it is one of the more boneheaded fallacies of the Method that actors believe they can tackle whatever role they like, no matter how unsuitable, because there is some trace of *every* character in the actor's kaleidoscopic make-up. That is one of those walloping great generalizations that sound persuasive until we begin to analyze them. It is true that in our "human nature" we all possess qualities of strength, cowardice, deceit, naivete, and all the other traits we associate with humankind, but it is wilfully obtuse not to recognize that certain qualities predominate and others are so slight as to be almost nonexistent.

If indeed every actor, because he possessed the full arsenal of human qualities, could play *anything*, then there is no reason why any actor could not be an Irving, a Booth, an Olivier, or a Scofield. It is the prominence of certain characteristics and the paucity of others that give actors their stamp of personality, and, though playing against the grain is a useful exercise in extending qualities not immediately apparent, it is doctrinal imbecility to ignore the unquestionable differences that make one actor suitable to play King Lear and another, the Fool.[1]

In the professional theatre, casting is determined mainly by readings or auditions of prepared material. (Although on the Continent, it is almost always decided by seeing the actor perform several roles in the current repertoire.) The reading is by far the most common practice and is preferred by both actor and director—unless, of course, it is a "cold" reading with the actor being tossed a "side" without time to examine the larger context of the play, in which case he thinks of it as an agony on a par with the Chinese torture.

The reading can be deceptive, for, as we all know, a fluency in reading does not in itself connote an ability to evolve a three-dimensional performance, and in this day and age, when actors take classes in order to master the technique of cold readings, its implications are even less reliable. The audition piece can be just as deceptive, as any actor with time and care can polish a three- or five-minute fragment into an impressive solo turn and still be woefully inept at interacting with fellow players in material not custom-made to his personality.

Both readings and auditions can be only tips of an iceberg that give very little insight as to what an actor can or cannot do. We must start by asking what, ideally, is the director trying to find in the casting process? If he has any sense, what he mainly is looking for is an aptitude towards change—not simply what the actor can solidify and deliver, but how he can alter and adapt what he *has* delivered according to new ideas proposed from another standpoint. The true audition is a test of both the actor's flexibility and his susceptibility to suggestion. His physical attributes, his size, shape, color, and bearing, are clearly visible as soon as he steps onto the stage, so two-thirds of the intelligence being solicited about him is immediately available. What is being sought now is some information about the mentality and expertise that lurk behind the physical presence—some insight into how those wheels go round and what makes them spin.

Audition methods vary according to the qualities being sought. A director looking for improvisational flair will learn next to nothing from a set piece of *Henry V*. A slice of Noel Coward will not reveal an actor's ability to take a role out of Miller or Odets and saturate it in telling naturalistic detail. A heavy piece of Camus will give almost no indication of an actor's facility in playing Congreve or Wycherley. By requesting "contrasting pieces" (a standard British procedure), the director hopes to uncover more facets of the actor than can be found in one monologue; but these are all so many veils, and unless the director pulls down the whole falsifying framework of the audition ritual, he will learn nothing: or, more to the point, only what the actor wants him to learn—which is the tiniest fraction of the full equation.[2]

The most strategic consideration in casting is the Compensatory Factor—that is, that psychological insufficiency in an actor's make-up that seeks to be compensated in the act of performance. On the simplest level, consider the case of a shy and repressed individual who turns to acting in order to experience an extraversion denied him in his personal life. That, for generations, has been one of the prime motivations among performers, much more so than the urge towards exhibitionism, which allegedly drives the showoff and the egotist onto the stage.

In the same way, there is in the secret center of every actor a desire to experience some fulfillment denied him in his private life. A shaky and indecisive person may find himself most fully realized playing the role of a highly assertive leader of men. A woman brought up in a severely strait-laced convent atmosphere may experience an inexplicable release playing an immoral woman of loose character. A rigidly organized person may find a peculiar elation in the role of an anarchic clown, a character whose world view is the antithesis of his own.

I am not simply talking about opposites attracting. The Compensatory Factor is much more complex, because usually the actor himself is unaware of what kind of compensation his nature is hungering for. He would have to possess an acute awareness of his personal psychology in order to discover which role would release those hidden springs that run beneath his social self. It is the kind of perception that, when ceded, usually belongs to an outsider. Sometimes, by accident, an unpredictable juxtaposition of elements comes into play, and suddenly we experience one of those revelatory performances where critics and public alike exclaim: "I never thought he had it in him!"—a perfectly understandable astonishment, as the incongruity of an actor's success in a highly uncharacteristic role is the result of wholly unsuspected secret affinities.

The Compensatory Factor is the antithesis of typecasting, as it flies in the face of the belief that "a certain kind" of person is best suited for "a certain kind" of role—a belief based almost wholly on external considerations. Nor is it in any way related to the Method fallacy that any actor is capable of playing any role—a mindless application of a democratic principle to an aesthetic realm where it does not pertain. The value of discovering this Compensatory Factor is that by unleashing an actor's profoundest feelings, by retuning his entire instrument to a higher or lower pitch, it produces a performance result whose effect can be dynamic: not just a reasonable facsimile or an impersonation sustained by technique, but a kind of rebirth of the actor within the microcosm of the unexpected character. We are always looking for this in the theatre: a combustion of personal and aesthetic elements that transcend the artifice of play acting. It is the underlying objective of rehearsals and the elusive pot of gold that we suspect but rarely discover at the end of rainbows.

Although it is difficult to command such a result, it is possible to intuit it, especially if in the audition process the director is using methods that employ contradiction, obliquity, and incongruity—that is, if the director is probing not only what the actor is putting on display but what the actor, out of ignorance or fear, is concealing.

An audition piece is often an elaborately woven mask that the actor, sometimes over a period of years, has managed to wedge—skintight—over his face. Its removal may make him highly vulnerable, which would be a first step towards discovering the face behind that mask. He may become distressed by the idea of exhibiting himself without the comforting illusion that he is projecting that personality that shows him off in his best light. Constantly, the director must strip away those concealments that the actor believes to be the mainstay of his art—not, one must add, to leave him naked and vulnerable, but to discover the true nature of the man and therefore the full scope of his talent.

Too often, an actor is merely an accretion of manners, habits, affectations, and personal quirks derived from more established actors of his own generation. In the twenties, there were hundreds of Barrymores—just as in the fifties there were thousands of Brandos and

Deans. The actor, emulating role models, unconsciously *imitates* them, as well, and one of the first objectives of actor training is to expunge those acquired characteristics. Given the brevity of most auditions, drastic measures are needed to catch a glimpse of the man who may be marooned behind the manner.

If auditions are a dilemma for the actor, imagine the situation from a director's standpoint. He is looking at the actor as if through a stereopticon slide—focusing his image of the role and his image of the performer to see if they can blend into one. He has *his* expectations, *his* preconceptions. He cannot be objective.

The actor, for his part, is projecting an image based partly on what he believes to be in the director's mind and partly on his understanding of his commercial potential as confirmed through previous employment. He is delivering that most painful of all performances—the projection of himself as he believes himself to be perceived by the outside world. At the same time, he is vaguely troubled by the inner contradiction that an actor is supposed to be an amalgam of different personalities depending on which facets of himself he chooses to bring to the fore. And so we have the spectacle of a man looking through blurred lenses at a man trying desperately to reflect himself in a distorting mirror. It is no wonder that actors rail against audition procedures and directors lament the fact that good actors are hard to come by.

In the case of new plays, the actor cannot hope to understand the predilections of a director's mind; more often than not, they have not even been formed. In the case of established works, the actor's conception of character is invariably conditioned by previous performances—perhaps those very performances that the director is intending to reverse as part of a fresh interpretation. It is not exactly the blind leading the blind, though it is certainly the confused leading the uncomprehending.

A certain amount of this joint confusion can be removed if the actor asks for some small indication of how the director sees the character, or, conversely, if the director volunteers a few words on the same subject. But the inviolability of the director's vision and the unspeakability of the actor's ignorance have become articles of faith in auditions. It is almost as if both parties are afraid of giving something away that might subsequently be used against them, and so what ought to be an open encounter between two willing artists becomes an awkward collision between strangers who, despite the exchange of civilities, rarely get acquainted.

The most one can hope to discover in an audition is the basic mettle of the actor's talent. As with the purchase of a used car, the director examines the chassis and notes the state of the paintwork, the mileage, the hum of the motor, the number of optional extras. He knows full well it will take days and maybe weeks before he understands the true state of the engine and how well or badly it handles on the road. Dutifully, the actor presents all his working parts along with testimonials from previous owners and papers elaborately documenting his service record. He has no inkling as to whether the director intends a short joy ride or a cross-country tour that will severely test the endurance of every mechanism. A spin around the block tells the director only the obvious things—how well it corners, how efficiently it starts and stops, whether its shock absorbers are working—but he can never know what it is like under pressure or how economical its gas consumption might be; that is, he can never know whether under the gun of concentrated rehearsal and constant abuse it will be capable of sustained high performance.

The basic components of a good actor are susceptibility to change, variety of expression, and sensitivity to rhythm. One simply must take for granted conscientiousness and technique. In the casting process, it is possible to test these qualities.

If an actor can take Hamlet's soliloquy "To be or not to be" and play it like a salesman hawking encyclopedias, like a professor delivering a philosophy lecture, like a sleepwalker under the influence of drugs, like a stand-up comedian belting out a nightclub act, like a chairman of the board delivering a statement to an annual meeting of stockholders, like a language teacher addressing a class of foreigners, he *probably* possesses a certain "susceptibility to change." If he can play it as a geriatric, a ham, an awkward adolescent, a lover, a psychopath, a ladies' hairdresser, and a gigolo, he *probably* possesses "variety of expression." If he can play it like a prize-fight commentator describing the exciting last moments of a heavyweight bout, a radio announcer being signaled alternately to slow down and speed up his weather forecast, a talking weight machine programmed to speak in strict iambic pentameter, a song-and-dance man rendering the text as a revue turn, and a surveyor measuring out a field in cubic feet, he is *probably* sensitive to changing rhythms.

Of course, and this is the rub, he can do all of these things supremely well and still be a bloody awful Hamlet. But if he is put through paces of this kind, the director will gain some small inkling as to what he can or cannot do—and if he is lucky, a great deal more about the performer's resilience, intelligence, and powers of concentration. Conducting an audition in this way tests that part of the actor where his creativity lives—the very part that will have to be activated in rehearsals. The audition should be as purposeful and precise as a doctor's examination, with the right questions eliciting pertinent information, the proper instruments testing the nature of all reflexes—no matter how inconclusive it may be about greater matters that can be ascertained only through subsequent trials.

One of the most dangerous audition practices is for the director to allow himself to be drawn into lengthy conversation with an actor, as there is almost no relationship whatsoever between an actor's intellect and his talent. One of Lee Strasberg's great failings as a director was his susceptibility to cerebral waffle—always believing that an intelligent and articulate actor would translate those conversational insights into his performance. He almost never did, and for weeks Strasberg would try to reconcile the mind of the man with the paucity of his talent.

We now know conclusively that there are nonconceptualizing actors who are almost incoherent but still capable of creating staggering performance results—results that are in no way diminished by the actor's lack of understanding as to how they came about. It is also dangerous to inspect an actor's resumé too closely, as that cannot help but cause us to prejudge the case. If we read that an actor has played Hamlet, Macbeth, Richard III, and Coriolanus, it would be natural to assume a certain degree of talent and expertise on that actor's part. Confronted by his subsequent inadequacy, it can sometimes take days to banish those erroneous impressions.

While we are on the subject of undue influence, we should be equally on guard against unqualified colleagues volunteering opinions on an actor's merit—either verbally or through the more deadly aspersions of body remarks, i.e., shoulder shrugs, eye rolls, nostril quivers, and raised eyebrows. Often when our own opinion is going through the delicate process of forming itself, a moronic stage manager or impertinent production secretary will hurry it into a mold for which it was never intended.

All unresolved questions concerning actors should be dealt with through callbacks—even if the process takes four, five, or six visits. Sometimes an actor's suitability establishes itself in five minutes, and when it does, the hunch should be acted upon immediately. Where there is uncertainty, the tedium of continued exploration is almost always worth the time it takes. Once an actor has been miscast, the mistake can usually be spotted in the first day's rehearsal. Anything less than a summary dismissal will open a can of worms, i.e, contradictory opinions, manufactured tolerance, hurt feelings, and sinking company morale, making proper work impossible.

The director must develop special antennae in order to spot the dilatory actor whose personal integrity, rhythm of work, or both make it impossible for him to produce quick results. If such an actor is made insecure or forced into expeditious short cuts, the director may never know the value of the treasure he has lost. There is a delicate balance between the actor who is slowly getting there and the one who is floundering and will eventually sink. Only the director's instinct can guide him here—although there is a natural point (roundabout two-thirds of the way into rehearsals) by which time the performance should be discernible. If there is no trace by then, it is unlikely to surface at the eleventh hour—although even that has been known to happen when, for instance, an actor on a wrong track is suddenly switched onto the right rail with a note, a costume change, or a radically altered piece of staging.

Finally, it might be appropriate to point out that the audition or casting session is one of the most stressful situations an actor ever experiences—far more painful than a first readthrough or an opening night. An actor at a casting call is a quivering concentrate of tremulous vulnerability. It is not his job that is at stake, but his life. Often, he comes to this Place of Judgment after several dozen rebuffs in similar places—his self-esteem in shreds, his despair tucked tightly behind his shirt front, his drooping spirit buoyed up for an encounter that may hurl him—yet again—ignobly into the dust. Sometimes these tremors of desperate energy fuse themselves into a creative outburst; more often they merely set off a series of underground quakes that shatter his composure and produce ineptitude.

The actor learns to cope with these hazards as the explosives expert does with land mines. Sometimes he defuses them and walks away smiling; other times, he is blown to smithereens. Audition stress is the actor's occupational hazard. It separates the men from the boys. It is no excuse to say, "Had I not been nervous, I would have given a marvelous rendering." Nervousness is the actor's ectoplasm. Nothing either good or bad happens without it. The professional has learned how to harness tension and turn it into energy. The amateur is constantly at the mercy of his hysteria.

At least that's what the director believes, and so, though he recognizes the stress of the casting call, he does not make allowances for it. Rather, he considers the actor's ability to control his emotions—or let them run away with him—an index of the actor's ability to perform. And yet, the same tensions that disfigure an actor's audition can, at some time of subsequent composure, underpin a brilliant performance. The most difficult distinction a director has to make is whether a flawed audition is a sample of the actor's norm or an aberration caused by exceptional pressure. There are no guidelines here—only the impressions gleaned from the debris of an actor's failure, and a judgment based on faith, instinct, and wild hunches. There are too many instances of great actors rising from the ashes of abominable performances for anyone to be smug.

NOTES

1. "As to the actor who 'plays himself,' I feel the opprobrium attached to such a criticism is extremely unjustified and testifies to a shortsightedness in those who bring it. All an actor can play is himself. Himself in the thousand-and-one variations dictated by a thousand-and-one roles. When people denounce a performer for 'playing himself' what they are really condemning is his basic shallowness and lack of personal resources. A multifaceted, substantial actor *plays himself* as relentlessly as does a spare and unendowed one. The resourceful actor, because he has more to draw on, will give the appearance of variety by simply utilizing the abundance of his nature. The resourceless actor, unblessed with such abundance, can do no more than exhibit his paucity in half a dozen slightly modified versions. The crime is not acting oneself, but not having enough of oneself to act!" (Charles Marowitz, *The Method as Means*, Citadel Press, New York). That was true as far as it went, but it blithely ignored the fact that most actors are not protean but limited. The exceptions (Olivier, Scofield, Richardson, Williamson, etc.) only prove the rule.

2. Joan Littlewood often forsook an actor's prepared piece and asked him to sing a song. Other directors ask the actor to tell the story of his life. I have occasionally requested an improvisation on the Lord's Prayer or a rendering of a nursery rhyme with a radically altered subtext (i.e., "Mary Had a Little Lamb" presented as a rabble-rousing political speech or an impas-

sioned plea for women's liberation). All of these departures from custom provide some flashes of the actor's uncamouflaged personality. Actors with facility for improvisation will seem to come off best, and sometimes better actors with no such facility will appear to be less gifted—an optical illusion to which auditions are highly prone.

4

The Interpreter's Wand

We call him a director, and we assume he "directs" the inner and outer movements of actors. We say that he "directs the play"—which suggests that he negotiates its movement from one place to another as if it were a bus and he a traffic cop. The "direction" of a play tends to suggest an angle of locomotion, and it implies that the direction taken, in another's hands, might be entirely different, might indeed be an *opposite* direction.

What these vague implications do not suggest is that a direction already exists—just as a trail exists in a wilderness if one can detect it among the bush and thickets. The play's direction is inherent in the play, and essentially, the director's work consists not of *giving* a direction but of *finding* one—the one that runs under the bush and thickets of the text.

In a great play—a play that offers several paths to follow, a play we tend to call a "classic"—the director's job is much harder. Here, he must seek out his direction using not only the play but the play's associations, and a play written in, say, the seventeenth century has acquired social, historical, cultural, and theatrical associations for some four hundred years. In a play such as *Hamlet*, for instance, everything we have come to believe about the character through criticism and countless stage interpretations becomes a factor available to the director. To speak, four hundred years after the fact, of the "original work" as if it still existed in its pristine state, is to ignore the changes and reversals that time wreaks on every living thing—and a play still performed four hundred years after it was written is unquestionably a "living thing."

I use the word *reversals* advisedly, because one of the most fascinating things about an old work written in a period when different moral and religious values pertained is the way in which something as basic as its philosophic outlook can be reversed. The notion of predestination, for example, is integral to Greek and most Elizabethan classics, but in modern productions of many of these works, this idea is glossed over or deliberately reversed. Free will is conferred upon characters whose actions were originally circumscribed by "the Fates." A classic that says one thing can, by dint of reinterpretation, mean something entirely different. To call that *mis*interpretation is to deny the ability of living things to change their nature with the passage of time.

It is only the hidebound academics who insist a play has one, unalterable meaning and who panic at the sight of that play *meaning* something quite the reverse. The one trait a classic has consistently displayed over the last four centuries is its ability to change identity in accordance with the way each generation has come to view it. Seeing Prince Hal as a jingoistic, war-mongering military hothead would probably have outraged Shakespeare, but given today's attitude towards chauvinism, it is a perfectly valid way of interpreting the character. Similarly, if a director chooses to view Hamlet as a social misfit, a spoiled brat, or a paralytic liberal mouthing empty platitudes, the text of the play will permit all of those un-Shakespearean permutations.

It is the malleability of a classic that we should celebrate, not simply its age; its uncanny ability to be (almost) all things to all men. Indeed, I am convinced that a play that is essentially unambiguous and resists diverse interpretation—although it can be a perfectly splendid play in its own right—will have less staying power than one that "alters when it alteration finds." *Death of a Salesman* is a marvelous play, and it will say more or less what it now says for many years to come, but I believe that a work such as *Waiting for Godot* will, in fifty or a hundred years from now, secrete shades of meaning that, were he alive, Beckett would fiercely reject. And it will be no less a work of art for doing so!

The act of interpretation is every bit as creative as authorship. The director, like the author, must marshal his arguments, structure his ideas, monitor the reach of his implications, and insinuate those meanings he wishes an audience to take away with it. In a classic, all of these things are done independent of the work of art, often as part of a superstructure built upon the foundation of the original work.

The director's task is further complicated by the fact that he has to organize his meaning through known characters and familiar situations that already mean something else to an audience. In that sense, he is never free of the original work, for even as he alters and rearranges the play's significance, he must be acutely aware of its *given* associations—what the audience is *expecting* it to mean. Without that knowledge, he will never be able effectively to reroute those meanings.

In *that* sense, he is working with more elements than the author. He is juggling the blocks of the play, its primal connotations, and the anticipations of the audience in regard to both. He is director not only of the actors in their search for new meanings, not only of the play's original intentions, but also of the audience's presumptions in regard to everything they already believe about the work they are about to see.

An original interpretation of an established work is predicated on certain insights that one man brings to the work of another. If he arbitrarily imposes ideas that have no bearing on the original and do not spring from seeds contained therein, he draws attention to himself in a very special way. He is inviting the audience to appreciate his opinions and insights at the expense of the work in question.

Even that can be construed as legitimate if those opinions and insights have freshness and originality in their own right, but if they are markedly inferior to the ideas expressed in the original work, he will be soundly trounced. For, in the case of Elizabethan, Jacobean, and Restoration writers, he is comparing himself with some of the keenest minds in English literature, and that kind of presumption, when it fails, produces the most violent denunciation. But if his ideas, no matter how innovative, can still be traced to motifs or assumptions in the original, he stands a better chance of bringing them off. A classic will accommodate almost any invention that still acknowledges its sovereign authority, but once a director denies that authority, once he loses radio contact with the original work, he is, in the most treacherous sense of the phrase, on his own.

Likewise, a playwright's relation to a classical work may be highly tangential and still pertain. For example, Tom Stoppard's *Rosencrantz and Guildenstern Are Dead*, despite its autonomy as a work of art, remains thematically related to *Hamlet* and still operates within the orbit of the original play. W. S. Gilbert's *Rosencrantz and Guildenstern*, being a parody and intended for quite different purposes, does not. Edward Bond's *Lear*, again an entirely original work, still feeds off certain ideas of class and cruelty that stem from Shakespeare's play, and so retains it as a reference point. Brecht's *Edward II* has a direct bearing on Marlowe's original, as does *Trumpets and Drums* on Farquhar's *The Recruiting Officer*. A certain far-fetched affinity pertains, in my view, even to radically different creatures such as *Kiss Me Kate* (*Taming of the Shrew*), *The Boys from Syracuse* (*Comedy of Errors*), and *West Side Story* (*Romeo and Juliet*), whereas the link is broken in works such as *Catch My Soul* (*Othello*) and *Something's Rotten in Denmark* (*Hamlet*).

In mise-en-scène, where the director is working with the basic material of the classic, it is much harder to free oneself of the gravitational tug of the original work, but as soon as a director's work ignores or unknowingly falsifies the ideology of the work, he steps beyond the permissible bounds of interpretation and produces the kind of gimmickry that fuels the arguments of the traditionalists.

There is, in certain works of art, a proclivity towards ideas and subject matter never considered by the author. For example, there are thematic strands in *Julius Caesar* and *Richard III* that enable modern directors to relate such plays to certain contemporary political events. In the thirties, Orson Welles easily tilted *Julius Caesar* towards the rise of Italian fascism with no injury whatsoever to the original work. Recently, in the Russian province of Georgia, the Rustavehli Company gave *Richard III* a relevance to modern dictatorships that, in a contemporary Soviet context, was both edifying and courageous.

There is, for example, in *Othello* a certain racial reverberation that may count for more with modern audiences than the crime-passionel of a Moor strangling his misunderstood bride. The anti-semitism in *Merchant of Venice*, a very incidental ingredient of the original play, is capable of being isolated and highlighted in the modern theatre in a way that would have seemed nonsensical to a spectator in Shakespeare's time. The antifeminist assumptions of *The Taming of the Shrew* (never considered as such in its own time) provide that play with social and polemical possibilities that actually alter its genre—turning a slapstick comedy into a grim tragedy about brainwashing and aggressive male chauvinism.[1] The magical properties of *The Tempest*, with characters such as Caliban representing our Id, and Ariel the personification of our suppressed desires, give that work a potentiality for Freudian interpretation that would have been as unthinkable in the seventeenth century as it seems logical in our own.

The fact that this subject matter did not (could not) occur to Shakespeare does not mean that it cannot (does not) occur to us. Nor does it mean that we are not entitled to act upon those impressions. At the bedrock of most of the plays we designate as classics, there are older works on which they have been modeled and, tracing back further, myths and legends from which *those* works have been fashioned. Our reinterpretations are part of the cycle. The Elizabethan age is as yoked to the mythology of the ancient world as the latter was to the primitive world that preceded it—as it is to the modern world, in which the same stories are unconsciously present and anthropologically embedded.

Reinterpretation falls into two general categories—either a director rearranges the emphases and inflections of the original material leaving the text intact, or he rejigs, restructures, and occasionally complements the original play with new material. Juxtaposing the world of the play, say, from one period to another, or, as in Peter Brook's *Midsummer Night's Dream*, from one visual ambiance to another, is the mildest form of reinterpretation, as a director is changing only tonality. Usually, in such cases, the altered framework sets the play into a new kind of relief, but the production does not alter its basic premise. Frequently, these productions are praised for their fidelity to the original, and directors are congratulated for "refreshing" the classic without undermining its integrity.

In the case of more radical recensions, the original work is the pretext for changes that are related (sometimes very tangentially) to the play's themes or implications. In the case of my own collage version of *Hamlet*,[2] lines and speeches from the original text were employed, but in an entirely different arrangement and in a sequence radically different from Shakespeare's. Since the starting point was to try to convey the essence of the play without relying on narrative, the selected material was chosen in order to flesh out a completely different structure—one that deliberately had no continuity or chronological development. However, the ideas, attitudes, and characters of the collage were in every particular related to, or made comment upon, Shakespeare's original.

In my adaptation of *Othello* and *The Shrew*,[3] contemporary scenes were added to chunks of Shakespeare, producing a stark, stylistic contrast between "classical" and "modern" that obviously was no part of the author's original intention. But again, the ideas incorporated through the new scenes amplified certain ideas triggered by the original work—so that no matter how oblique they may have been, there was an intellectual connection between the play's ideas and the contemporary views imposed upon them.

One must say at once that structural change bears no relation whatsoever to originality of interpretation. It does not follow that a drastic reordering of a text bestows startlingly new dimensions. Sometimes it only draws attention to arbitrary stylistic devices that add no new meanings but convey only a certain air of novelty, whereas a genuine reevaluation of values within the formal limits of the work as originally written can produce an astonishing sense of newness. (Of course, "newness" is neither the priority nor the objective but the consequence of reconsidering the *donnée* of a given work, perceiving it differently.) The great distinction to be made is between surface change and thematic originality. Too often a classic, jazzily costumed and freakily bedecked, is the oldest of wines in the fanciest of new bottles. A fundamental shift in the basic strategy of a classic can be made with minimal surface change or none at all. Sometimes, of course, a new set of externals is the inevitable consequence of a new way of dealing with a play's components.

One ought, at this juncture, to mention those alleged reinterpretations of classics that are nothing more than the misguided modernist's rebellion against tradition. Several years ago in New York, Joe Papp presented a version of *Hamlet* that, by flamboyantly declassicizing the work (intruding slang and street language), tried to imply a kind of "No More Masterpieces" approach to the text.[4] It was, of course, preposterous, and was rejected as such. Pique, impotent rages at convention, desperate bids to *épater le bourgeois*, or fatuous attempts to try to change the fashion are never legitimate pretexts for directorial interpretation—although in the presence of a truly original conception, all of these things come into play. Unfortunately, we look to critics to protect us from grandiloquent frauds, and they are often the people most readily taken in.

Describing ways in which a classic can be rethought on the stage would be tantamount to giving lessons in original thinking—a pointless, not to say presumptuous, exercise. But there are some hints on this subject that may be worth conveying in order to describe the mental processes by which an interpretation might assemble itself in the director's mind.

If, as we leaf through the pages of a classic, some inexplicable connection develops between a contemporary allusion and the material that has given birth to it, rather than dismiss it as whimsy or coincidence, we should follow the lead to see if it opens up new territory. If, for example, it occurs to us that the dying world depicted in *Macbeth* has something apocalyptic about it, and that Macbeth's demise is not just the defeat of a soldier outnumbered by opposing odds but the annihilation of a certain universal order (precipitated, perhaps, by the murder of Duncan, whose life and reign exemplified the Well-Ordered State), we may be on the scent of a kind of post-nuclear vision of Shakespeare. (We may also be on the scent, one hastens to add, of one of the most common clichés in theatrical mise-en-scène: the tendency to give seventeenth century classics a modern, nihilistic twist.)

But danger of cliché notwithstanding, it is certainly feasible to reorder the events of *Macbeth* in such a way that they imply a terminal phase of our own civilization. The strength of such an interpretation depends upon the aptness of our parallels and the deftness with which we reinvent the characters of the play. If, for instance, we can visualize Macbeth's blood lust not merely as the ill-fated designs of an ambitious general but as the renunciation of all moral sentiment, a return to that more primitive period before Christianity and learning began to refine human conduct, it is possible to see the play as the end of a certain civilized order. The witches, by some stretch of the dramatic imagination, might be portrayed as those doomwatchers in the Pentagon who monitor the number of warheads accumulated by each side and drily report the narrowing odds in favor of nuclear holocaust.

If we manage all of that, we still have the problem of Birnam Wood to solve, and here, the literalness of Shakespeare's image does not fuse easily with a metaphysical approach. And so, stage by stage, we discover that we cannot simply immerse the play in an unqualified generalization—spread sauce, as it were, over the body of the play to alter its flavor. Rather, we must (if you will permit the mixing of metaphors) butter each piece of its toast separately.

A director of my acquaintance found in *Coriolanus* a parallel to the rise and fall of General De Gaulle. Each had an excess of pride, he pointed out, and each was destroyed by it. When his "interpretation" was put to the test, he found he couldn't match his models. The play's logic simply did not reflect a historical parallel with postwar France, and too many factors refused to assimilate. De Gaulle was not dominated by his mother as Volumnia dominates Coriolanus, nor did the president's arrogance resemble Shakespeare's Tribune, who actually loathes the rabble. (De Gaulle, of course, loved "the people" and consciously played up to them.) Finally, there was no immediate parallel to Aufidius, and so the battle scenes had nowhere to go other than in the direction Shakespeare originally intended.

I cite this untenable case because it is not sufficient for an actual personage merely to resemble a classical character. The implications of historical events either have to dovetail with the classical narrative or diverge in such a way that some point is made that is relevant to both storylines. Occasionally, without attempting anything so specific as a parallel, a character can be projected as a jacked-up, theatricalized version of the original—as, for instance, De Gaulle himself was depicted in Edward Wilson's T.N.P. production of Jarry's *Ubu Roi*, a work that lends itself both to caricature and, given the tyrannical world in which we live, to topical allusion.

A Rumanian director I once knew had an ingenious conception of *Hamlet*. He postulated that the ghost who coaxes the young prince into all his deadly embroglios—arranging the murder of his old schoolfriends, stabbing a respected old court councilor, causing the death of his mother, and eventually dispatching Claudius—was, in fact, Fortinbras in disguise, and that the purpose of exhorting his "son" to revenge was deliberately to bring about all the personal and political calamities that paved the way for his own succession to the throne.

No doubt, a production of *Hamlet* can be mounted on that premise, but it would produce the same effect of cleverness as contained in this description. It is, at a pinch, reconcilable with the events of the play and could be made plausible, but it does not enlarge or enrich our understanding of the work. It has all the surface dazzle of an ingenious gimmick, but none of the unfolding illumination and considered implication we look for when a traditional work and a contemporary outlook march hand in hand.

Classical reinterpretation, particularly in Europe, has become something of a trickster's art. Having demonstrated that Shakespeare's works can be permutated, the tendency is for directors to outdo one another in mounting unexpected inversions of them. That has infuriated traditionalists, who have used such productions as a stick with which to beat down all innovation. A new kind of virtue has been cast on the solid, straightforward Shakespearian revival that eschews "tricksiness" or novelty and drills assiduously into the marble of the original text. It is a dispute in which we often find ourselves championing a trend even as we castigate its chief exponents.

Gimmickry and novelty, for their own sake, are constant hazards in all play production and not restricted to the revival of classics. But traditionalists are on weak ground when they insist that Shakespeare should be allowed to "speak for himself"—as if there were a feasible way for actors, directors, and designers simply to posit the collected works without the intercession of artistic imagination and personal choice. Even the most faithful exponent of Shakespeare's works is obliged to filter the writer's meaning through his own understanding, and like it or not, the only voice Shakespeare has is the one through which his interpreters speak—and *everyone* is an interpreter.

We may cavil against liberties taken with the text, departures from traditional readings, impositions of what appear to be extraneous ideas, but when we come right down to it, every actor and every director of whatever stamp is coloring the work with his own palette. Too often a "straightforward" production is simply one in which the meanings of the scenes are not rethought or tested anew but simply are repeated as they were in former productions. Solid, straightforward, square-footed Shakespeare is frequently the verse with the poetry left out—or the story minus the point of view that gives it dramatic pertinence.

The most faithful way to perform Shakespeare is to bring to the plays the same volume of crackling energy and imagination that Shakespeare himself brought to the stories he was refashioning. To be as full of invention as the author of the plays is perhaps the most quintessential Shakespearian approach a director can adopt. What is deadly is the belief that the plays' greatness is "automatic," and all one has to do is push a button and they will immediately clatter to life. There is nothing automatic in art. Every moment, if it's to have any value, has to be wrung out of some measure of creative agony. "Easy art" is perhaps the greatest of all contradictions in terms.

In a theatrical world where new plays, new styles, and new fashions frantically compete for attention, the lodestar of a classic becomes more and more important. To be able to rely on a work of art's flexibility to correlate a modern sensibility to the experience of former times is what makes possible the continuity on which culture depends. It is our precise knowledge of the archipelagoes of the past and the fact that they are accessible by jetliner or space shuttle that prevents "man" from becoming "an island unto himself."

It is entirely to the innovator that the classics owe their survival in the modern repertoire. Meyerhold, Tairov, Coupeau, Vilar, Barrault, Jouvet, Planchon, Stein, Besson, Strehler, Brook—these and directors like them are the vigilantes who have refused to allow the old works to become mildewed and predictable. The surest way to kill a play is to mount it with uncritical respect and fail to find that new bud on the old branch that gives it a special pertinence to a modern audience. "The difference between the present and the past," T. S. Eliot has written, "is that the conscious present is an awareness of the past in a way and to an extent which the past's awareness of itself cannot show."

Through the medium of contemporary theatrical interpretation, a director is able to revive a classic in such a way that "the past's awareness of itself" not only can be shown but can be made to enter into a dialogue with the present, thereby shedding new light on both present and past.

NOTES

1. See *The Shrew* (Marion Boyars, 1976).
2. *The Marowitz Hamlet* (Penguin Books).
3. *The Marowitz Shakespeare* (Marion Boyars, 1978).
4. "No More Masterpieces" is an influential essay from *The Theatre and Its Double* by Antonin Artaud, which encourages the demolition of long-established and reverential works of art.

The Designing Director

5

A man writes a play. It contains an implied vision of the world he has created. Another man, the director, reads it. He conjures up another vision. A third man is given the same play. In him, yet another vision of that world is evoked. He is then told to "design it"—that is, to take his vision, coalesce it with the visions of the other two men, and materialize it.

Since each of the three men in this process—the writer, the director, and the designer—tends to be creative in his own right, it is foolhardy to expect the three separate visions to combine as one. The playwright, according to the unwritten rules that govern play production, relinquishes *his* vision of the work as soon as the director creates *his*, and the designer, if he is worth his salt, brings his own distinctive view of the whole. From the outset, three visual conceptions of the work compete for precedence. As soon as actors are brought into the equation, additional notions of style, shape, and color arrive with them.

Which vision ultimately dominates depends on the weight and influence of the respective collaborators. An established director with a clear personal view can usually call the tune. Sometimes, if the strongest member of the triumvirate is the playwright, he can insist on the supremacy of *his* vision. More often than not, because a certain kind of politesse tempers all power struggles, the designer's conception is compromised by the needs of the director and the preferences of the playwright. Sometimes, where a star designer is involved, the director gratefully accepts his visual concoctions and adapts his production accordingly.

What I have described is the way these things usually work in the professional theatre. Each collaborator provides a slice of the cake, and critics, in recognition of the fact, proceed to assess each slice separately: the play did this-and-that; the director did such-and-such; and the designer did so-and-so.

The ideal, from the Duke of Saxe-Meiningen through Stanislavsky and Gordon Craig up to the present, has always been for a unified vision—the director's—delineating all aspects of the production so as to endow the final result with homogeneity. When a director works with a dead writer, Shakespeare, for instance, his autocracy over the production's design is not questioned. It is assumed that his interpretation of events and relationships includes his idea of the way things look. It is also assumed that his view of the play (the playwright not being available for consultation) is the only one with which the production need concern itself.

Occasionally, the ideas of an ingenious designer will impinge on this conception, but usually the director holds sway, and everything is subjugated to his will. When Peter Brook both directed and designed *King Lear*, for example, the setting was predicated on a visual conception inseparable from the play's interpretation. In *Midsummer Night's Dream*, although Sally Jacobs was credited as designer, again what materialized on the stage was inextricable from Brook's overview of the entire work. In fact, when any director is fortunate enough to possess an overall concept of a play, the settings and costumes are integral to that conception, and, whether doled out to an individual collaborator or executed by the director himself, they "belong" to the director's view of the whole.

To this assertion, a chorus of irate designers can be heard crying: "Heresy!" Their argument goes something like this:

The designer, like the director, is a creative member of the partnership that realizes the final work. His contribution, no less than the director's or the actor's, is a vital ingredient in the totality that becomes the final work of art. Like the director's, his imaginative input is pertinent. Like the actor, he too has an interpretative part to play. Like the writer, he too has "ideas" about the theme, the mood, the meaning of the play.

Viewed this way, the playwright provides, as it were, the trapeze on which the director, the designer, and the actors are invited to "do their stuff." But is a play really as loose and free-swinging as a trapeze, and can it accommodate the grip of anyone who wishes to take hold of it? Of course not! A play has its own parameters—and although these may contract or expand depending on the talents of the collaborators at work on them, the play is not clay to be shaped to the will of each consecutive member of the artistic team. Nor is it, to demolish my own simile, like a trapeze—empty until filled with an acrobat's performance. Those who are dead set on analogies perhaps should think of the playwright as the architect of a swimming pool. The director fills it with water and then invites his collaborators to dive in. Once in the water, whatever strokes he and his fellow artists choose to make, he is swimming in the writer's element and within boundaries fixed by the original work.

The designer always rises in prominence in direct relation to the director's lack of visual expertise. But if a director is able to conceive the visible world in which the play takes place, why does he need a designer at all—except to provide the tangible details of his vision? What he really needs are the skills of the builders, the architect, the painter, the seamstress, and the sculptor. However, he doesn't need them *in their own right*, but only insomuch as they help flesh out his vision. Indeed, if he gives them free rein, if he allows them to "express themselves," what can they express but ideas alien to his own?

A production is not a parliament with everyone entitled to a vote, but a dictatorship in which members serve the higher will of one man, the irony being that he himself is serving another—namely, the playwright. Paradoxically, to the extent he serves the writer successfully, the director is pursuing his own ends, but it is because those ends are prescribed by the playwright that even the most autocratic director is prevented from ever becoming a despot. A despot imperviously imposes his own will and is the sole arbiter of all events, but the director imposes his will for the sake of the tyranny imposed *upon him* by the play. Try as he may, he can never escape the stranglehold of the play.

Adaptation, fragmentation, extrapolation, even distortion are all needle fluctuations within the compass of the original work. The only way the director can ever burst through the confines of that work is to author it himself. Being the "author of the production" (a common phrase to describe the director's work) is a misnomer. The *author* is the author of the production—although it may be the director's penmanship that everyone sees. A production is, so to speak, *already* authored by the man who wrote the original work and set its course in one direction rather than another.

Although the director, sometimes by a flamboyant display of his talent, may persuade people that he is the production's driving force, that is a misleading impression. A "directorial concept" is only a translator's tool in rendering the ideas of the originator, and even when an approach is taken in direct opposition to a work's basic assumptions, it remains an inversion to be appreciated and understood by reference back to the original—just as, for instance, the theological disposition of Protestantism, despite all its reforms and different perspectives, takes on definition only when referred back to Catholicism. Indeed, one could look at Luther as the innovative regisseur of Christianity: a man who developed an interpretation of the Gospels radically different from the way he found them being practiced in the sixteenth century. The fact that he split the church and founded a new one is, in terms of my analogy, less pertinent than the fact that he did all of that with transmutations of traditional material that continued to exert its original appeal centuries after Luther's innovations had taken root.

The set designer has three options: he can try to visualize what the director has in mind; he can try to persuade the director to accept his modifications of that vision; or he can try to foist a personal work of art independent of the intended mise-en-scène. Often the latter is the more brilliant design qua design, but as it is disconnected from the life of the production, it doesn't matter. Its brilliance will only emphasize its irrelevance to the greater design that is the production.

More often than not, the designer opts for the second course and, within the limits set by the director, attempts to insinuate his originality and invention. If he is supremely gifted, he will take the first course; that is, he will defer his personal invention and fulfill in *his* realm what the director has conceived in *his*. In so doing, he will be exercising his art to the highest degree, as it is much more challenging for a designer to find the play's imagery through the eyes of the man who is translating it on stage than to impose imagery of his own.

In practical terms, the collaboration the director enters into with the designer is almost identical to the one made with the actor. As with the actor, he is dispensing imagery in the hope of conditioning the work he will be getting back. A sensitive director will no sooner propose sketches of his ideas for a designer than he would render line readings or inflections for an actor. By pouring the appropriate verbal imagery into his ear, he should enchant the designer with the kind of world he wants him to evoke.

If his inductions bear fruit, the pictures the director begins to get from the designer will be a personalized version of that initial stream of imagery. The director, in a sense, is there to program the designer's dreams—to produce, by inference and suggestion, a graphic equivalent to his own flights of fancy. It is naive to believe that a designer's visual imagination can be stimulated only by pictures and diagrams. The history of novel illustration and representational painting of all ages attests to the fact that words are what propel the artist into imagery.

Having said that, I can recall an instance in which the method broke down. When I was preparing a highly political version of *Measure for Measure* for London, I talked to my designer about a huge legal scroll made of gauze, behind which Angelo's seduction of Marianne would be seen to take place. From the scroll, embossed with an old Latin law, the reigning idea of the play would issue unobtrusively throughout the evening. A legal scroll, I pointed out, symbolized the law in the popular imagination—papyrus, Moses' tablets, the Vatican Pronunciamentos, etc.

When we met for our next session, he had designed a stage chock full of legal scrolls—about twenty of them, twenty to thirty feet high. Rolled-up scrolls were leaning against the walls, beside the table, under the furniture: everywhere the eye could see. It took a long and painful discussion to point out the stark effectiveness of a single scroll hanging from the flies that would roll up and down like a miniature curtain, exposing the Latin calligraphy and insinuating the notion of "the law" in every scene.

The tendency of designers is to design, but nothing is easier than to create designs extraneous to the needs of a production simply because the tools are at hand and the inclination to use them is irresistible. Often, those "design ideas" are reiterating the mise-en-scène or stating in a bald frontispiece what the play will be saying as its actions accumulate. That is, perhaps, the single most common sin of stage designers: letting the whole stylistic story out of the bag before the actors have uttered a word.

What has been obscured in the practice of stage design is the subordinate connotation of the word *setting*. A setting is there to *set off* something else; its efficacy can be judged only when the centerpiece for which it has been created is put in place. For that reason, the best stage set is the one that is incomplete until the actors enter the stage to resolve it. A stage design that is breathtaking and glows like a finished work of art is almost invariably in need of revision when the performers "enter the picture."

A scale model of a stage design, the usual means by which the set is appraised by the director, can be a deceptive toy. In most instances, the scale model does not inhabit the larger framework that is the theatre; almost always, it simulates the dimensions only of the stage. And yet, the ambiance of the auditorium is an inextricable factor. It is in that ambiance that the public will experience the set and the actors bringing it to life.

Examining the scale model from an angle that does not apply in the actual theatre gives a distorted impression. A topographical view of a model in a theatre where none of the audience ever has a topographical view of the stage must be misleading. A parallel view of the same model in a theatre where the auditorium is steeply raked is equally misleading. In fact, even the best miniature scale models can produce an effect that is radically altered when the set is actually built and standing on the stage.

In the German theatre, there is a kind of mock-up design rehearsal long before the set is ever sent to workshops. In this *bauprobe*, a variety of flats, boxes, and other geometrical objects, identical to the intended size of the design, are placed loosely on the stage to enable the director and designer to gauge their effects spatially. Because these are actual masses on an actual stage, one can judge in a moment whether the intended distribution of space will work in conjunction with actors. The scale model and the *bauprobe*—cosmos and microcosmos—go hand in hand, each shedding light on the other.

Often the set designer is also in charge of costume design, but let us suppose, for the sake of argument, that these are two distinct offices executed by two separate individuals.

Usually, the costume designer comes to the first reading and, after his minions have taken the actors' measurements, disappears into his own inner sanctum until the final rehearsals—at which time he will reemerge to clothe the players and become the center of a stormy, and largely avoidable, controversy.

The notion that a designer, after a few inconclusive discussions with a director and a superficial exposure to the playwright's text, is prepared to create the apparel for all the dramatis personae is clearly preposterous. Barred from the development of character that is the objective of rehearsals (usually a self-imposed exile), the costume designer has no idea what changes are taking place in a character's personality and how these changes will affect his wardrobe. It is assumed that clothes are a priori choices, and the actor must simply assimilate them when dress rehearsals arrive. Although the actor, the playwright, and the director can afford the luxury of changing their minds through constant trial and error, the costume designer is expected to make final decisions before rehearsals begin and to stick to them no matter how radically the ground shifts in the meantime.

As a result, when dress parades come round, the actor is often forced into visual conceptions that have been modified or even reversed while the costume designer has been busily executing the pattern of everyone's premature decisions. If a character changes and develops in a four- or five-week rehearsal period, how can he be expected to fit snugly into the clothes decided upon before embarking on his journey? It is a little like asking a full-grown adult to squeeze into his graduation suit, and actors are entirely justified to reject those costumes that they can no longer reconcile with the people they have become.

What would make much more sense would be a process whereby the actor begins rehearsals in a sketchy and generalized costume that seems appropriate, and as he makes his character discoveries, he alters and discards those bits of dress that no longer apply—a process that should be rigorously monitored by the costume designer, who should be obliged to attend an average of three rehearsals a week. In this way, the actor's conception of character and the character's conception of clothes go hand in hand with the designer's conception of design. As the actor achieves those perceptions that, for example, may escalate the social level of his character or, conversely, reduce his social standing, the costume designer is at hand comprehending the reasons why X, originally thought to be an affluent dandy, is now revealed to be an impoverished trickster merely displaying affluence—a discovery that would subtly alter the cut, texture, and swathe of his costume.

I can recall an incident in a modern-dress production of *Hamlet* where the actor playing Horatio started out as an Establishment figure

close to the Danish throne and so was costumed in a vest and pin-
stripes—only to find towards the end of rehearsals that he had become
a social misfit at Elsinore and was now obliged to wear jeans and a
turtleneck. The gradations by which his character transformed were
entirely logical in terms of the production's progress—although they
didn't seem so to the costume designer, who had created a splendid
three-piece pinstriped suit that fit to a T and was then told to go out
and buy a pair of faded jeans and a sweater. The fault was not hers,
but that of the system that had banished her from the crucial artistic
considerations that necessitated the change.

It is because costume is thought to be the province of the designer
rather than the actor that it remains one of the most volatile areas of
collaboration. The actor, at the height of those conflicts, invariably
cries: "I'm the one who has to wear the bloody thing!" It is an irre-
futable argument, and because it is, the actor, in conjunction with the
director who has brought him to that pass, should be the final arbiter.
But in the professional theatre, dress tends to be thought of as the
costume designer's "opportunity to express himself," his "claim to
fame"—as with the set designer, who in *his* arena feels entitled to
brandish his own personal showcase. So long as theatre continues to
be thought of in those terms, a parceling out of creative opportunities,
a departmentalizing of a process that ought to be unified, it will continue to incite useless controversy and exacerbate the war of egos to
which it is, in any case, helplessly prone.

The history of stage design was written not by the set designer
but by the director. Jessner's stairways, Appia's painting with light,
Meyerhold's constructivism, Piscator's mechanized, multimedia stage,
Brecht's Epic Stage, Artaud's spectacle surrounding the spectacle, all
were tangible expressions of the director's quest for visual means to
convey dramatic purpose—which is not an attempt to belittle the
achievements of the designers who produced those settings, only an
attempt to put them into perspective.

What do we mean when we refer to a "stage design?" Assuming,
of course, we do *not* mean a picture painted on a stretched canvas
intended to suggest the locales in which the action takes place; that
is, assuming we do *not* mean what stage design of the nineteenth and
early twentieth centuries meant.

A design is primarily a dispensation of space; secondarily, a structuring of that space; and thirdly, a selection of objects, material, and light incorporated into that space to interact with people. These are the most vital considerations of theatrical art, too vital to be delegated to designers. They are the aesthetic choices that the playwright insinuates upon the director, and even then, they are largely unconscious and exist *between the lines* of the work being performed. The writer's interest in them is proprietary—not managerial. He owns the lease on the terrain where the work is taking place, but he is neither its architect nor its builder. These tasks must be subcontracted if anything of worth is to stand on his land—even though, in every case, it is his wishes that are being carried out.

The dynamics of the Elizabethan stage conditioned the whole of Elizabethan drama. No matter what scenic effects, costumes, and settings the play contained,[1] the basic distribution of space—a jutting forestage, an upper stage, two side stages—was the crucial design from which everything else followed. Once the theatre was forced inside the picture frame, spatial design was superseded by scene painting.

The "design" of the eighteenth and early nineteenth centuries consisted largely of configurations behind a picture frame, the crucial design being the stage itself: a box into which designers were encouraged to insert a variety of painted tableaux. One of the most dynamic stages of the early twentieth century was Jacques Coupeau's Vieux Colombier (allegedly designed by Louis Jouvet), and, like all startling innovations, it represented a return to earlier forms—in this case, the Elizabethan stage. Coupeau's stage—an open acting area with a trapped forestage, an upper stage, and wings leading directly onto the main area—was the *donnée* upon which directors and designers were invited to adapt everything else. There is something eminently sensible about a stage design that says: "Here is the basic structure on which all our work will be done." Choose any permutation you like; it doesn't matter. The fundamental design statement having been made, it will accommodate anything you wish to say. You will never contradict the essential statement that the stage *is* a stage and not a "box" to house replicas and reasonable facsimiles.

Theatrical art needs to lay down architectural principles before it can begin to "say" anything. Indeed, the design of the theatre speaks before the playwright does. The Restoration stage said from the outset: "Here is a place where language and posture are primary." The nineteenth-century stage said: "We will dazzle you with pictures." Coupeau's stage said: "Here is a bare platform on which we present the actor's art." Even when the stage was filled with set pieces and decor, it remained a stage designed primarily for the actor's art.

In the theatre, the architectural *medium* is very much the *message*, and the actor-audience relationship is constantly affecting the nature and purport of that message. The angle from which a spectator views a performance, for instance, profoundly affects his attitude to the theatre experience. A show viewed from a high gallery not only is more physically remote, it is dramatically distanced, as well. The gulf between the performance and its perception renders it less accessible, in actual terms, than a performance whose closer proximity engages the spectator's active participation. As a result, the distance from the spectator becomes what it was never meant to be, a stylistic factor, objectifying an experience intended to be close and personal. The spectator sitting nearby in the stalls experiences shades of feeling unavailable to the gallery-goer. He is privy to more dramatic information than his "distant relation"; consequently, his experience—depending on how far from or near to the action he is—radically alters the complexity of the story being told. Denied subtlety and the impact of subtext, the gallery-goer interprets only the broad outline of a performance and responds only to that language which "gets through" to him because of its volume or repetition.

Of course, the question that is begged here is: What should the appropriate size of a theatre be? In my view, musicals and spectacles notwithstanding, no theatre should seat more than five hundred, and no auditorium should fan away from the stage farther than sixty feet—the general rule of thumb being no more than three times the depth of the stage.

The question that is never asked in oversized theatres (because commercial considerations would panic at the answer) is: How far can acting project without losing touch with itself, that is, before it becomes a physical semaphore conveying only bald, dramatic information?

There are many answers to that question, depending on whether the projected material is Chekhov, Shakespeare, Rodgers and Hammerstein, or the intimate ambiance of a one-man show, but generally speaking, my reply is that beyond sixty feet, the actor is forced to cut that vital link between interior truth and his technical projection of it. Once it is cut, something begins to issue from the stage that is akin to acting but spiritually divorced from what we traditionally mean by the word. A vocal and kinetic transmission takes place that, paradoxically, *overplays* that which is no longer in touch with the essentials of playing—namely, the actor's controlled sensitivity to inner states and the dissemination of meanings beyond those literally contained in the text. "Overplaying" is yet another of the theatre's misnomers. It projects something beyond the range of what, artistically speaking, one would call "playing," and, as a voice straining to be heard can no longer be called "speaking," so acting that strains to communicate beyond the strength of its own transmitter produces a din that can no longer be called "acting."

In the twenties with the experiments of the Dadaists, and then again in the sixties with Happenings, the entire realm of stage design was temporarily liberated. It became clear (particularly in the sixties) that what had been hemming it in was the strictures of the playhouse. As soon as performance freed itself from the playhouse, as soon as dramatic scores—rather than plays—were essayed in public squares, on rooftops, in warehouses, in department stores, etc., all questions of stage architecture and "aesthetic distance" vanished. In their place was a spate of new spatial possibilities that owed nothing to the traditions of theatre design.

It was a short-lived breakthrough. It lasted for about twelve years. The conservative instincts of playgoers insisted upon the comfortable confines of the upholstered auditorium, and by the 1980s, the memory of Performance Art in alien surroundings and the whole paraphernalia of Happenings seemed cloyingly déjà vu. Occasionally, so-called environmental productions would continue to transform the venues of certain theatres, and audiences would be regaled by the non-theatricality of unfamiliar trappings where previously they were accustomed to a rigid demarcation between audience and actors, but by and large, the theatre (apart from traditional outings into the open air) remained cloistered inside the eighteenth-century structures that, with minor modifications, made up our twentieth-century playhouses.

The freedom only touched upon by Happeners, the Environmentalists, the Action Painters, and the Performance Artists is certain to resurface in the not-too-distant future as the tantalizing possibilities thrown up during that period continue to be exhumed.[2] Its most telling experiments, the work of Alan Kaprow, Ken Dewey, Claes Oldenberg, Jim Dine, and Jean-Jacques Lebel, influenced largely by the aesthetics of John Cage, were inspired and in the main executed by artists—sculptors, painters, assemblagists, collagists, etc. What theatre practitioners there were took their lead from these artists and never quite equaled their more sensational events. What emerged clearly from that period was that theatre could subsist without the support systems of playhouses and the ministrations of traditional theatre workers. (Almost no actors took part in Happenings; the artists preferred to use what they called "real people.")

More important, it became apparent that the actual venue, if properly chosen and intelligently implemented, could add dramatic dimensions with which no conventional theatre could compete. The associations that cling to a public site such as Trafalgar Square or the Pentagon, an automobile graveyard, a suspension bridge, or a clearing in the forest, cannot begin to compete with artistic reconstructions in a 40×40 square wedged at the end of a raked auditorium. The Great Designs, one realized, already existed. They were out there in the world beyond the playhouse waiting to be appropriated by adventurous theatre artists.

An extratheatrical performance has distinct advantages. It increases the range of experience available to the public and frees "drama" from the stranglehold of the writer. In a large, open area, for example, theatre artists are obliged to look for bold ingredients: sights, sounds, crowd dynamics, and mixtures of these, beyond the conventional impact of language—ways of expressing emotion and depicting character that push the actor beyond the narrow limits of psychology and verisimilitude. Imagery *must* be larger than life; actions *must* transcend the stilted two-step of naturalistic behavior.

Theatre of such size and on so great a canvas encourages the creation of a vocabulary that goes beyond the tired accents and recycled clichés of written dialogue. The quest is no longer towards linguistic expression (i.e., more telling ways to say things that in any case have been said a thousand times before) but towards a concrete language of sight and sound whose syntax has not yet been formed; towards, in fact, the kind of theatre proselytized by Antonin Artaud but that he could never bring about using the fluffy tools of thirties surrealism.

In this century, every major breakthrough in the theatre has been a movement away from the conventional playhouse. Constructivism was merely a way of disguising the stage by rearranging its planes and surfaces; arena staging, an asinine attempt to demolish the fourth wall by eliminating the other three as well. (All that did was emphasize a fact abundantly clear in the proscenium theatre—namely, that the audience is an indissoluble party to any dramatic action.) The thrust stage, the railway stage, and the apron stage, by encroaching upon the audience's preserve, merely brought the old stage conventions into a different proximity with the audience but in no way altered the dynamics of the traditional relationship.

Indeed, so long as spectators and performers share the same interior geography, it matters not a whit how the space is divided up or what it is filled with. The old bond is broken only by confronting the public in areas where there is no vestige of the old spatial relationship, and hence none of the ingrained psychological associations that cling to it. A performance area, which is not a contrived setting but a chosen locale for the instigation of dramatic events, *becomes* a theatre in the way the old tavern-yards of the middle ages became theatres simply by housing a wagon and a makeshift platform. The concentration of artistic forces on the site conjures up the events, and because the old connotations no longer apply, the possibility of fresh expression exists.

Of course, even in a square, a park, or a field, or on a mountain plateau, some trace of the old spatial relationship reasserts itself. Bring five hundred people into an open field, start to play, and they will form themselves around the action as instinctively as the early pioneers attacked by Indians made a circle out of their wagon train. But if the physiognomy of the performance space militates against an involuntary return to the old forms, and if the action, instead of being centered, is distributed into various areas, and if simultaneity takes the place of Aristotelian continuity, and if it is not a "story" that is being transmitted but a juxtaposition of dramatic strands that yields narrative only *after* the event, there is a good likelihood of a new kind of dramatic experience being ceded.

Here, the director is not merely a monitor of speech and blocking, an arbiter of rises and crosses, but a coordinator of fundamental theatrical ingredients—sound, imagery, mass, color, rhythm, psychology, fantasy, physics, and metaphysics. He no longer tests inflections or suggests readings. The interplay of character is only one small part of his great design, which is equally concerned with the relativity of mass, space, distance, and motion. And, he also becomes the "director" of a whole host of exciting new "extras"—those extratheatrical random factors that come about because of the redistribution of his formal structures. Improvisation takes on a completely new meaning—no longer loose wadges of hastily evoked dialogues that approximate the writer's invention, but the spontaneous commission of existential factors such as movement of crowds, the cross-blending of one action with another, the incorporation of accident and surprise, the acceleration or reduction of tempi, depending on a slew of spontaneous occurrences that, though prepared, can never be "rehearsed."

That, you may say, is as far removed from design as it is from direction—and yet it only seems so, because it is removed from the customary context in which these arts usually perform. Once we have freed ourselves from the idea that a director is someone who sits at a makeshift desk in the middle of an empty auditorium, and a designer is a man who supervises technicians in a workshop to insure that they are properly executing his blueprints, the entire pursuit of dramatic art is put onto a different footing, and, if we are lucky, its products no longer resemble the predictable artifacts of the past.

Theatre artists are constantly clamoring for "new forms" and "new modes of expression"—even as they are gathering together their flint and stones, wrapping animal hides around their middles, and using their fingers to daub paint on the walls of their caves.

NOTES

1. And the idea that it was largely a bare stage is a fallacy brilliantly exposed by Lee Simonson in his book *The Stage Is Set.*

2. The two most distinguished anachronisms from that period now at work are Robert Wilson and Richard Foreman.

6

The Rehearsal Process, or "Gloucester's Leap"

Describing the essentials of orchestra conducting, Otto Klemperer once said that one of the most important things was to let the orchestra "breathe"—to allow the musicians to play in rhythms natural to themselves rather than being constantly orchestrated by the conductor.

This idea is as important to actors as it is to musicians, because the ultimate objective of all "direction" is not simply to receive back from actors the instructions given them by the director but the amplification of those instructions enriched by the actors' talent and imagination. Once the notion behind a scene has been insinuated and the dynamics suggested, it is the act of actors "breathing naturally" (i.e., playing spontaneously) that fulfills or frustrates the director's design.

What is involved here is not so much "direction" as *activation* of certain parts of the actor's personality over others—for instance, encouraging a mildness where a raucousness is being offered, or an intimacy of tone in place of the bluster an actor has mistaken for earnestness. Often the requisite qualities already exist in the actor, and the director need do nothing but give them their head. The unique elements in an actor's performance, those qualities that "breathe naturally" because they are part of an actor's personal constituents, can become immobilized if the director draws attention to them. Sometimes the most acute direction consists of those things the director has the good sense *not* to discuss. The most natural course for an actor is for him to apply his talent to the real problems of a role and leave the tractable stuff alone.

There are innumerable instances of artists' creating artificial problems, then earnestly tackling them, totally unaware they are uselessly diverting energy. I have witnessed hours of discussion about the color of a dress or the shape of a sideburn while "in the meantime some necessary question of the play [was] then to be considered." Perhaps unconsciously, people are aware of the irrelevance of these preoccupations and use them to divert attention from crucial problems that are much harder to solve. A neurotic preoccupation with externals is almost always an indication that something central is being overlooked.

The director is the litmus paper on which the actor tests his ideas. Unless the actor receives some kind of affirmation of his legitimate results, they will dissipate in endless experimentation. A rehearsal breakthrough doesn't need a monument erected in its wake, but if it is not acknowledged in some way, the actor has no measuring rod with which to gauge his progress.

There is a kind of director who simply posts himself at rehearsal and sits there like a recording mechanism, his face never betraying a trace of value judgment. When he does speak, it is merely to describe what he has seen actors perform, to trade civilities, or to ooze encouragement. It is as if his presence is merely the wax into which the actors are cutting their performance, but as it is taking place without the ministrations of an engineer, it is very likely to produce distortion.

It is always distressing for actors to feel that a director is oblivious to their changing choices, just as it is gratifying for them to sense that he is perceiving and grading each subtle variation. When actors designate a director as being "bad," they often mean nothing more than that he was absent in that delicate, collaborative process during which each should be answerable to the other.

Throughout that highly charged rehearsal period, when the actor and director are silently jockeying for position, it behooves the director to understand the delicate nature of his collaborator. Often, there is an unconscious resentment on the actor's part in altering his conception to fit the director's instructions (an understandable resistance against acknowledging a creativity greater than his own), and so it is useful for the director to adopt an oblique approach. A direct criticism that forces the actor to abandon a cherished but misconceived idea is far less effective than an observation to another player that by implication contains the same criticism.

For example, if I want to tell Actor A that he is too emotionally effusive, I may ask Actress B to see whether she can find a way to subdue the intensity of the scene. Whatever Actress B does with this direction, Actor A will get the message that the temperature of the scene is too high, and that may well mute his performance—perhaps on the pretext of trying to help Actress B achieve a change in her own adjustment. Although that may seem a devious way with which "by indirections" to "find directions out," it has the benefit of prodding the actor to solve his own problem in his own way, and that is always more effective than direct impositions from without.

The director has to make sure that he is leading, not trailing, the actor. Frequently, a director fired by a bright idea asks for just that effect the actor has lobbed into the performance. That has to shake the actor's confidence in his director. The director must be able to ascertain whether he is instigating the actor's idea or simply parroting it after the fact. Because of the intimacy of the relationship (the actor and director threading a path through the same underbrush to the same clearing), it is common to confuse the other's initiative with one's own.

The director is looking for a result—frequently verbalizing it; the actor is also looking for a result—trying to intuit it through the material. A declaration of the desired result, no matter how articulate, may be precisely the factor that militates against achieving it. Many actors, recoiling from the dead tradition of Delsarte, are too sensitive to give the director precisely what he is asking for—not because they cannot, but because it flouts some unarticulated principle that holds that the actor must not be a puppet, nor the director a puppet master.

The cliché of the crude silent film director calling out "joy," "fear," "terror," "love" while an obedient artist rings the changes, haunts every actor's imagination. He knows that emotions cannot be summoned, as it were, by numbers, and instinctively resists any attempt to mechanize what should be an organic process. That is why slyness and taciturnity are sometimes the director's most effective tools. You can bring a horse to water, but you cannot make him drink—whereas you can, by ingenious methods, so engender the craving in the horse that he not only finds his own way to water but with such an irrepressible thirst that nothing will prevent him from slaking it. Although the deviousness that we associate with child psychology is anathema to many actors, the act of play production is akin to child's play, and much of this kind of psychology applies.

The tendency of the actor, no less than the director, is for short cuts, the justification always being the pressure of time. But a short cut is as insipid and nonnutritious as the battery-hen egg compared to the free-range variety. There are certain shorthand terms from which neither the actor nor the director can escape: *slower, faster, louder, softer.* A negative connotation has sprung up around these words, and for some artists, their use is incontrovertible proof of a crude and inartistic temperament. Although this distaste can be carried to extremes (because sometimes the use of a simple dynamic term is precisely what is required), the fact remains that this theatrical shorthand is too imprecise to satisfy the demands of the rehearsal process. If a tempo is not slow enough, it has to be "even slower," although "not *that* slow" but perhaps "just a little bit faster"—like trying to regulate the trickle from a faulty water faucet, it will involve endless twistings of the spigot.

The advantage of making directly for the core of a scene's intention without concerning oneself about tempi is that the actor is given a skintight leotard that will assume whatever shape his body demands. By finding the true center of a scene's meaning, the actor has built into his performance not only the appropriate dynamics, but the parameters within which those dynamics may legitimately range. Therefore, a performance played slowly one night or faster the next never violates the core center of the scene, even though its rhythm varies considerably. True dynamics can never be imposed; they grow out of the needs of a performance and the performance's own need to alter somewhat from night to night. Precision is a virtue in the execution of business and the timing of lines, but a straitjacket when imposed upon the emotional quantum of a living performance.

Finding both the general rhythm and the general size is part of the same quest. Often the actor has to experience excess in order to achieve moderation, to feel what "over the top" is before he can identify playing "on the line." I conducted experiments along these lines in London in the early seventies, and only years afterward did I learn that they resembled the "law of reverse effect," a psychiatric technique developed in the late 1930s by Viktor Frankl. Being overanxious, Frankl found, often produced precisely those adverse effects that caused a patient's condition. A person who worried about stammering, stammered all the more, but when asked by Frankl to do so in a school play, the stammerer found himself unable to. A bank clerk who required legible handwriting in order to maintain his position became obsessive about it, and his handwriting began to deteriorate, but when Frankl urged him to try to write badly, the condition cleared up.

In acting, the "law of reverse effect" is particularly useful in highly emotional scenes where the actor has either the fear or the tendency to overact. By encouraging him into excess and overstepping the mark, the bogie is exorcised. In rehearsals, he experiences the whole-hearted self-indulgence of an overstated performance, and because it is openly acknowledged as such, it is discharged from his system. The same principle applies in the case of heavy or villainous characters (i.e., Claudius, Iago, Richard III, etc.). By being forced into extremes wherein their evil is broadly caricatured, the actor is able to begin to step back to a more moderate mode of performance. Having tasted the sourness of excess and exaggeration, he begins to look for and appreciate the flavor of a more subtle characterization.

The director creates a basin in which the actor may freely swim. The measure of his success is directly commensurate with how much scope he provides the actor, and how much restriction. Getting the balance right between a performance's freedom and its form is where the art of the director lies. Because he is working with that most variable of all factors—the human being—he has to allow for fluctuations. But because he is working in an art form that depends upon decisive structure, he has to imply design. It is because contradiction lies at the heart of all theatre that the director has to be the master of thesis and antithesis; the defender of freedom and the vigilante of form.

A rehearsal period is like a "ronde" dance that has to fit to a specific length of music. In the early stages, when there are still plenty of measures left, the company can afford to try one step after another, but at the close, the dance and the music finally have to come together.

The pressure of time (often felt in the very first days of rehearsal, although it should not be) has to be balanced with the patience required to make discoveries. There are two fatal courses in the theatre: making decisions too soon and making them too late. Most people err on the side of the former. The actor wants to settle on his result as quickly as he can so that he has plenty of time to polish it. Consequently, he often arrives prematurely at conclusions that turn out to be misguided. He is then obliged to discard them and start again.

There is no correct time to settle on the true significance of a moment. Each rehearsal period dictates its own rhythm. There comes a time when something simply is right—not because it has been crowned with laurel leaves or awarded a gold medal but simply because it has been quietly taken for granted and the work has proceeded to the next stage. It often happens that later findings suggest reversals of these earlier choices. Rather than throwing up our hands in horror, we should celebrate such backtracking, because it usually means former decisions have been based on false premises. The underlying quest of rehearsals is not only to discover the validity of present choices but to confirm previous ones. Nothing can be finally settled until the whole is settled, and so as with a crossword puzzle where correct new words force out erroneous ones, the end is inextricably connected to the beginning.

The actor (and particularly the Method actor) spends a great deal of his rehearsal time "making choices"—as if he were shopping in a vast dramatic supermarket. The assumption is that if one "choice" doesn't work, he can always replace it with another. It rarely occurs to him that choices, in order to be pertinent, must originate from a general conception that tallies with the spirit of his material, and that if this wider conception is missing, he can "make choices" till kingdom come and still have nothing to show for it. A "choice" must not be equated with a lottery draw. It cannot be made without reference to a fundamental grasp of theme and character. Once a performance is properly harnessed to the underlying matter of a play, it is astonishing how many "choices" are automatically eliminated. It is when the general intellectual framework is not grasped that the actor experiences the heady freedom to "choose" to his heart's content; to indulge, in fact, in random choice, which is pointless within the framework of a play whose scope and intentions are clearly prescribed.

In a production of *The White Crow* in Los Angeles, I worked with an actor who made and discarded choices as if he had an unlimited supply of the things. But if a choice such as "I am weak, frightened, and wary" can be replaced with "I am strong, defiant, and aggressive," there is surely too much leeway to admit of definable character of any sort. Hamlet, for instance, can be many things, but he cannot be decisive, inarticulate, and unreflective and still inhabit Shakespeare's play. If a turn of 360 degrees can be made so blithely, there is no character foundation upon which to build. Indeed, the whole concept of "character" implies the existence of one set of characteristics to the exclusion of others.

As rehearsals mesh the theories, hunches, and suppositions of all concerned, many things will be thrown up. The emergence of a mistaken idea enthusiastically supported by the actor but clearly invalid, must be stamped down the moment it appears—despite the wounds it may inflict on the actor's ego. An interpretative fallacy, if it is allowed to fester, infects everything around it. If it is temporarily condoned, it will be twice as difficult to remove later on. An actor respects the swift, sharp dispatch of an inconsistent idea because it implies the existence of a value system on the part of the director. Although he may not know what is required at a given moment, he knows instinctively what is incompatible with the interpretation, and by tossing it out of court, the director delineates the frame of reference by which the actor may judge all subsequent ideas.

The gorgeously democratic notion that "everything is worth a try" is potentially deadly if the director knows full well that a particular suggestion is so irrelevant that it could never in a million years harmonize with his conception. Despite the impression of despotism it may create, the director is well advised brutally to expunge the quirky, the deviant, and the extraneous, no matter what ill feeling that engenders. However, I must add hastily that if there is a smidgen of sense in an actor's suggestion or the remotest possibility it might open a door or unseal a window, it should be granted its stage time. The distance between a valid experiment and a pointless waste of time is sometimes that of a hair's breadth, but the director must carefully gauge the density of that strand.

One of the prevailing clichés about rehearsals is that they are "voyages of discovery." Although in one sense that is true, it is worth noting that any voyage that ever discovered anything worth finding set out with some kind of map of the territory, no matter how primitive.

Too often, rehearsals are not so much "voyages of discovery" as they are reconnoitering missions—just to see what is out there. Unless a director has shared a general conception with his actors, and each member on board is aware of the purpose of the voyage, a lot of time can be spent just meandering. Often, setting out with no clear view in mind, the cast hopes blindly that the play will steer them to the proper port. That is, of course, deadly, because a production without a purpose is the exact equivalent of a ship without a rudder.

It is never enough to assume that the play will lead the way. The best of plays must themselves be led by the interpretative skills of the

company coalesced to some kind of directorial vision. Actors and directors often abrogate their responsibility by failing to realize that
without their creative input, there is neither form nor content, and
that a play, no matter how tantalizing its potentialities, remains inert
until they breathe life into it.

I do not intend thereby to belittle the work of the writer, for
clearly, unless the potential for art is contained in the script, there is
nothing to realize in the first place. We also know from the consistent
and consistently atrocious performances of so-called classics that the
certification of quality in an established work of art is no guarantee
that its interpreters will match its greatness.

A new play is even more problematic. There are many instances
of plays that have foundered in their first productions only to be
salvaged in later ones. That was the case, for instance, with Tennessee
Williams's *Summer and Smoke* and O'Neill's *The Iceman Cometh*.

There has to be an equivalence between the virtues of a written
work and the talents of the people trying to express it. I remember
the British playwright John Mortimer telling me that he would not
consider the production of one of his plays unless a particular director
was available to mount it, so certain was he of the affinities between
his script and this person's vision of it. In the commercial theatre, it
is often the case that certain "vehicles" bide their time, sometimes for
years, until a desired star actor is available for them. Getting the chemistry wrong because one has mismatched either actor and director or
director and writer is often fatal in the theatre, because, more often
than not, a play doesn't get a second chance.

The text, the moves, the timing, the actions constitute the tangible
elements of the production, those parts that must be perfected
through repetition (i.e., "rehearsal" in French *is repetition*). But beneath
these elements runs a current of energy that is equally important.
This energy, the protoplasm that gives these tangibles their living
texture, is nourished by improvisation. Improvisation, the free play
of imagination on the prescribed elements of the play, provides the
heat that brings all these other ingredients to the boil.

Improvisations have three main rehearsal functions. By inventing
and acting out situations referred to in the script but not actually
written, they amplify the partial view of characters and events that is
all a play can ever provide. They fill in the event by giving actors a
palpable experience of what might have preceded the scenes they

actually perform. Second, by providing these implied experiences, they extend a character's behavior in such a way as to broaden the scope of his characterization. They literally provide the past upon which the present is predicated, thereby enabling the actor to arrive chronologically at the events he is to portray. Third, by suggesting parallels to the situations depicted by the author, they provide a test for the veracity of human behavior. By playing out invented situations similar to those provided by the author, they can show up implausibilities or inconsistencies in the text, thereby instigating relevant revisions or amendments.

But their greatest virtue is that by encouraging free play among actors, they prevent material from becoming stilted and bloodless. An improvisation restores the bubbling individuality of the actor. By throwing him back onto his own impulses, he is better prepared to adapt himself to the needs of his character. By recontacting his own feelings, he is freshly reminded of how they pertain to the character he is attempting to enliven.

Improvisations that correspond directly to the material as depicted in the play are both redundant and intimidating. A playwright has already made those moments concrete with text and actions that usually cannot be improved upon by an improvising actor. Then what is the point of trying to create an inadequate approximation? An improvisation, to have a point, should probe areas in the scene not already treated—moments that pertain, no matter how obliquely, to the actions already provided so that the actor is constantly widening the scope of his material.

If an actor has a block in relation to a particular scene, it is useful to relax the playwright's hold on the character and encourage the actor to find alternative (even contradictory) ways of treating the given material. In Strindberg's *The Father*, there is a scene in which the captain confronts his loathing for Laura and delves into those past events that crippled their relationship. In the same scene, Laura recognizes why and how she came to love, and subsequently hate, her husband.

It is a difficult scene in which some volcanic emotions are released, and in a production of the play I directed in Norway, the actors found it virtually impossible to reach that stage of cathartic realization that the play demands. At first, we improvised parallel scenes—scenes of similar traumatic revelation in the characters' lives; then we tried acting out the past incidents described in the speeches—all to no avail. Finally, we hit upon the idea of treating the horrific, wrenching confessions as meaningless levities—as they might be recalled by the same characters thirty years hence in their dotage.

By relieving them of the immensity of their conflict—by, in fact, diminishing the import of those terrible admissions—a new perspective was achieved. A lightness of tone, a kind of weird black comedy crept into the material, which, although irrelevant to the direct needs of the scene, enabled us nevertheless to return to Strindberg's situation refreshed and unconstricted. The absence of lightness, it turned out, was precisely what had made our previous work so stilted. Although not exactly transformed into comedy, the scene gained a certain detachment that helped to objectify its somewhat psychodramatic elements and, eventually, achieve an equilibrium.

Not every scene problem is susceptible to remedy through improvisation, but when the absorption of character has become all-consuming, a return to the actor's founding personality is sometimes the best way of refreshing the character's persona.

The other attribute of improvisation is that by inviting the actor to display his own creativity, it relieves the grim, relentless atmosphere that often turns rehearsals into feckless labor. Rehearsals should never feel like factory work, even when their main purpose is only drill. Sometimes the introduction of improvisation is the equivalent of a holiday from pure technical slog, and, more than a coffee or smoke break, it is important for the actor to have an art break—to refresh those parts of himself that delight in invention, flights of fancy, or sheer ostentation. A rehearsal that feels like a chore, though it instills some useful pattern of staging or memorization, dampens the divine sparks by which actors must live.

The rehearsal process never ends. It goes on even during coffee breaks and dinner intervals. Every moment of communication between the actor and director is an opportunity for artistic interchange, even when the conversation appears to be trivial or irrelevant to the work at hand. Just as a scientist sometimes hits upon his most inspired formulae when he is far from the laboratory, sitting under a tree or flying his kite, so the best of the actor's insights may come to him outside of rehearsals.

A director should never underestimate the power of an idea—a perception about a character or a scene that can sometimes spawn an entirely new creation. If a picture, as the Chinese say, is worth a million words, then the introduction of a new idea is worth a million stage directions. A provocative idea, one that jolts an actor's imagination into an unexpected new direction, is like that piano that Irving Berlin had constructed for himself by which, at the flick of a lever, he could transpose the key of any melody he had composed. The practice of theatre is predicated on the execution of specifics, and direction that is not couched in specifics is of no use to an actor. That being the case, imagine the usefulness of an idea that already contains a wide range of specifics and needs only to be suggested in order for a transformation immediately to take place.

In a production of *Hamlet* that I directed in a German theatre, the actor's preconception of Claudius was mentally rooted in the persona of Joseph Stalin—a furtive, wary, suspicious tyrant who ruled with an iron fist. That ran contrary to my own conception of the role, but it was virtually impossible to alter the course of his characterization. In a long, nocturnal discussion after an equally long German meal, I persuaded the actor to substitute for Stalin the image of Konrad Adenauer, a strong, authoritative head of state but with somewhat more democratic leanings than the Soviet leader. Within hours, the performance had begun to transform, and my attempts to eliminate those traits related to the actor's earlier model began to bear fruit.

Had I tried to remove each specific gesture and mannerism related to the previous conception (as indeed I *had* done for a while), I would have got nowhere—as the actor had set his character, as it were, in the key of C, and I was constantly suggesting sharps and flats that did not belong in that key. But as soon as the key signature itself was changed, all the new chromatics came along with it. One idea had become the equivalent of several dozen specific "directions," and a fundamental interpretative shift had taken place.

Whether he verbalizes it or not, almost every actor models his role on some figure, real or imaginary, that in a sense "directs" him from the inner recesses of his mind. This Ur-Character, as one might call it, may be at odds with the character the director is trying to create, and he would have no way of knowing it. The director, of course, has his own Ur-Character, and he is assuming that the actor is helping him to realize it. But that is a naive assumption, for just as a play provokes imagery in the director's mind, so does it in the actor's, and no matter how much an actor presents himself as a tabula rasa, if he is any kind of actor at all he is being motivated by personal preconceptions.

In that sense, the rehearsal process has strong parallels with psychoanalysis, in that the director (analyst) must penetrate the actor's (analysand's) unconscious at least so far as to bring into open the actor's hidden choices. Just as the stumbling block in an analysis is the patient's unwillingness to confront certain unpleasant truths about himself, so the problem in rehearsals can sometimes be the actor's repression of choices about which he is ashamed or reluctant to speak. If, for instance, an actor identifies Lear with his own intensely disliked father, the resentment born of that relationship will become a factor in the performance. If a director wishes to expunge it, he will be obliged to trace it to its roots—and since these are in the actor's unconscious, it is useless merely to tamper with the externals of style and stagecraft.

As soon as the director realizes that working with the actor means entering into a relationship with shifting degrees of consciousness and unconsciousness, he comes into that arena where practical work can be done. Too often, such considerations are dismissed as irrelevantly "psychological," and the director proceeds to parcel out only those external aspects of his actor to which he has easy access—all the while extolling the virtues of "professionalism" and technique. That is merely toying with symptoms and ignoring their cause. Usually, although certainly not always, it is a futile practice. The director must be perceptive enough to realize where the root of a theatrical problem lies—whether in an actor's technique, comprehension, personality, or psyche. Wherever it is discovered, that is where it must be rooted out.

The parallels with analysis go even further. The director, hiring the actors, giving them instructions, automatically assuming compliance, cannot help but be an authority figure, and the actor cannot help but regard him as such. We know from almost a hundred years of psychoanalysis that at the root of many behavioral problems lies an individual's relationship to authority figures, surrogate parents, etc. The actor's dependence on the director is often as great as any experienced in his childhood. In the case of celebrated or strongly opinionated directors, the actor makes almost no move without first obtaining permission. Even as he fends for himself, he is constantly looking over his shoulder for signs of approval or disapproval. And, as with parents, the force of a rejection is as wounding as a compliment can be euphoric.

During the course of rehearsals, the director consciously uses his power to approve or reject. He must also make himself aware of how his actors respond to such charged emotional dispensations. If too great a dependence is built up in an actor, he may never be able to cut loose and realize the individuality of his role. If he is inwardly rebellious, the entire rehearsal period may be an endless series of frictions.

Giving orders is second nature to directors, but taking them cannot be entirely normal to full-fledged adults who have already broken traditional ties with their parents and discovered their own selfhood. The contract between actor and director (both legal and customary) is that the director will command and the actor obey, and that remains so even when there is great cordiality and mutual affection. Because it is obvious, actors and directors tend to play down the hierarchical aspect of their relationship, preferring to emphasize collaboration, evoking the image of colleagues working evenly hand in hand. But the fact remains that the conceptualizing instinct of the director is constantly molding the actor's performance towards his own ends, and, despite the appearance of parity and independence, the actor knows he is expected to follow another's lead.

The acceptance of directorial authority is best achieved when the actor sees eye to eye with the director's interpretation. Then, the actor is simply concurring with a fellow artist on how the work is to proceed, and, accepting the play as the central authority, there is no subjugation involved in the relationship. But if the actor's view diverges from the director's, the difference of opinion can trigger a complicated pattern of resistance that has to do only ostensibly with questions of interpretation. Resistance in the rehearsal process is of two kinds: there is the actor's divergent view of the material founded on intellectual or emotionally based objections to the interpretation, and there is the transference of irrational feelings to thwart the will of a figure who, in the actor's unconscious, stands for someone else.

In the case of the first resistance, the director may be the recipient of new and startling insights he has not had the prescience to have himself, and the tension is healthy and creative. In the case of the transference, the director, like the analyst whom he resembles, must find a way to make the actor distinguish between personal obsession and artistic discretion. He cannot do so by launching an analysis in the midst of rehearsals, nor is he qualified to deal with problems on that level. And so he must do the next best thing, which is to use the play as the objective criterion with which to justify his case and convince his actor. That may mean having recourse to the opinions of others in the cast, to scholarly sources, to drama criticism, to the general consensus, etc.

In such a case, the director is put in the position of an advocate forced to argue his case for the sake of the recalcitrant actor. By constant reference not to his hang-ups or his unconscious drives but to the logic and unity of his own conception, he may bring the actor around. Commanding his obedience will only strengthen the transference and cause it to become even more solidly entrenched. Gentle, firm, or even emphatic persuasion with reference to the common object is his only hope.

Some readers scanning these words might well smile to themselves and muse: "Why not just fire the fellow and hire another actor?" Of course, that is a common solution to such problems, but overriding an actor's resistance and winning him over to a viewpoint he initially found untenable produces a performance result rich in texture and electric in tone. The greater the distance an actor has to travel to a legitimate result, the more complex and fulfilling that result will be.

The rehearsal period, like the analysis, is trying to penetrate mysteries, many of them unconscious, in order to alter behavior. The actor, by probing the background of his character, is trying to achieve a oneness between the playwright's creation, the director's interpretation, and his own conception of character. The analysand's "blocks" and the actor's preconceptions about character are almost exactly analogous. In each case, a presumption about self has to be altered in the light of new findings—in the analysand's case, those thrown up from memories of childhood and symptoms of everyday life; in the actor's case, those unearthed from improvisation, character analysis, and the director's observed connections between the script and the ways in which the performer acts upon it.

The great advantage in approaching the work in this frame of mind, a quest to be achieved rather than a set of givens to be represented, is that it activates the right set of muscles in the actor, those that incline him towards invention and discovery. It may seem surprising to those who possess an idealized view of the dramatic process, but what is most often responsible for failure in the theatre is the fact that the actor does not accept his work as an invitation to creativity but merely as a time frame in which to project those traits and mannerisms that he displayed previously. In his mind, *who he is* rather than *what he can become* is the reason for his being cast.

Since Stanislavsky (which is to say since Freud), it has been impossible to deal with acting problems without also dealing in psychology. Certainly long before Stanislavsky and Freud, the same kind of exploration was being conducted by actors and directors without recourse to fashionable phraseology. Even Richard Burbage had to deal with "motivations," "complexes," and "repressed desires," although I doubt he actually used any of those words. Our modern investigations into the mind are additional tools in the work of the theatre. They are not a panacea—either in art or in life—but that doesn't mean we shouldn't use them where they seem to apply.

The great danger is to assume that these are the *only* tools we ever need—which is like assuming that behind the secrets of the human heart and mind, psychology is all there is. Even the psychologists know that to be false. The director who is really doing his job is as open to sociology, anthropology, politics, religion, the occult, physics, metaphysics, and nuclear physics as he is to the Method or Brecht's theories of Alienation. As with a sophisticated computer, the appropriate disc must be inserted to help solve that problem to which it pertains.

Some argue that the most strategic member of the theatrical collaboration, more important than actor, writer, or director, is the public.

It is unquestionably true that a performance without a public is like tennis without the net. The presence of the public determines the veracity or mendacity of a production's choices. However, it is a determination that the artists premeditate and, to an extent, decisively influence. It is conceivable that a production can make all the right choices and still have no impact with the public. It is equally true that given that lack of impact, all those choices can be altered so as to induce audience response—although, in so doing, the spirit and character of the work will be betrayed.

In one sense, the public is the arbiter of the artifact, but in another, it is entirely up to the artists to determine the proof of a play's propositions. To reorder those propositions to achieve public approval is as reprehensible as to rig them in the first place. There are too many historical instances of obtuseness on the part of the public for us to make it the final arbiter. Of course, commercially, there is no usurping its authority. But artistically, it has a strong susceptibility towards misunderstanding, resistance to innovation, and stupidity in the face of nonformula, groundbreaking art that upsets its expectations or threatens its composure. Viewed from a historical perspective, the public is always right—unless, of course, it's the wrong public, in which case its judgments are drastically reversed when the "right" public comes along.

The actor's most irresistible tendency is to play the whore with an audience. Confronted with indifference or lack of response, actors instinctively overplay, drop their pants, or beg for love. There is nothing like "a bad house" to bring out the worst in actors. Indeed, the audience is often the most deleterious influence an actor has. To satisfy it, to "win them back," actors will abandon all sense of degree, forfeit all credibility, and violate every intention painfully implanted during the rehearsal period. A negative shake of its collective head, and every aesthetic idea to which actors had been staunchly committed for weeks flies out the window.

A director, no matter how brilliant, no matter how great the loyalty he has been able to muster, no matter what unanimity has been achieved in rehearsal, cannot compete with a groundswell of disapproval. A negative rumble from a first-night audience, and he is peremptorily dethroned. The actors' insecurities, methodically overpowered during rehearsals, come flooding back to drown the director as soon as audience reaction begins to question his authority. No one is thrown to the dogs more quickly, and no bones are picked clean with greater delight than his.

On the other hand, should a director spend several weeks vainly trying to win over a recalcitrant cast, becoming in the process the most contemptible figure since Judas Iscariot, and should the public subsequently acclaim his efforts, no coronation is quite so swift or splendid. The alchemy by which an unpopular director garnering golden notices suddenly becomes a hero to his company is enough to dizzy the senses and turn a Seventh-Day Adventist into an agnostic.

It should be borne in mind that the director is also subject to stage fright. He too can panic, lose his cool, find himself relying on tricks of lighting or sound, lapse into arbitrary groupings or movements for their own sake. He is just as prone as the actor to "ham it up" or indulge himself at the expense of the script. He is just as liable as anyone in his company to "lose his lines" and desperately improvise. That is why in a healthy company a system of checks and balances applies. Sometimes it is the company that must direct the director back to the proper path, and, if an atmosphere can be created in which deviations can be checked without too great a loss of face, it is the best of all possible worlds.

Once we have acknowledged the innumerable personal styles of individual directors, we are drawn to the conclusion that, essentially, there are only two modes of direction: the Laissez Faire and the Faire Comme-Ça.

The Laissez Faire method is by far the most popular with actors, in that it encourages them to perform comfortably and is based on the assumption that the actor gives and the director receives. In this relationship, the director is merely a convector for the actor's heat, and there is a tacit assumption that he is not to interfere with the natural flow of the actor's invention. Here, the striving for directorial goals, no matter how legitimate, takes a back seat to the actor's ingenuity. Inherent in the relationship is the notion that the actor is the dominant partner, and the director a kind of grateful recipient of his efforts. Although "production" certainly takes place, in that the director performs all his conventional tasks, it is always from the standpoint of a monitor rather than an arbiter.

Under the Faire Comme-Ça method, the director formulates a specific blueprint that the actor is then expected to realize—whether in keeping with his personal inclinations or not. The goals of the interpretation are usually set higher than the actor's reach, and the success of the work depends precisely on the degree to which they are achieved. More important, the actor is encouraged to assimilate and execute ideas that are outside his immediate frame of reference, ideas that are germane to the director's conception of the play as a whole. That is, the director working from a master plan expects the actor to raise himself to *his* standard and refuses to accept results, no matter how "natural," that fall short of that mark.

In the course of this dispensation, rehearsals are often turbulent and filled with stress. Comfort, ease, and "playing naturally" are qualities that do not gain easy access. The quest for goals beyond the actor's immediate range tends to discommode him; the comprehension of ideas not personally arrived at rattles his composure. It is an approach that infuriates the "coasting actor" who relies on customary mannerisms and proven effects in order to "get by." It demands an intensity of concentration that many actors do not associate with professional work, which, over the years, has acquired social corollaries such as "enjoying one's self," "getting on with fellow artists," and engendering "no sweat"·situations. It is the antithesis of lazy acting, as its results are wrenched out of the kind of artistic agony that precedes the creation of any work worth watching. For all these reasons, it is a modus operandi that is simultaneously romanticized and avoided.

Throughout their work, there is a constant struggle for supremacy—the actor resisting ideas he finds unconducive, the director imposing ideas he believes to be vital. In a healthy relationship, neither artist is so fixated that he cannot concede the persuasive ideas of the other, and in a proper working relationship, there is a golden mean that persuades both partners to accept antithetical ideas that seem appropriate to the overall design.

But this golden mean does not come about by magic. It must be cultivated from the first day. The proper aim of rehearsals is, gradually and progressively, to delineate an intellectual framework that will validate certain ideas and invalidate others. Again, that does not happen of itself but is the inevitable consequence of the directorial overview. It is this overview that determines the difference between right and wrong, because it provides a context in which all choices can be assessed. The absence of such a context (that is, the absence of a collectively understood governing idea) leaves rehearsal choices to the mercy of dominant personalities and endless contention.

When things deteriorate to the point that artistic rights and wrongs are determined only by vociferous arguments between rival egos, it is clear that there is no production concept worth preserving. It is best then to dissolve all the constituents and start again—the one course of action that is almost never taken, because, by that time, the exigencies of openings and the dogma of cost insist upon resolution, no matter how disastrous.

What then becomes clear from an extended analysis of the rehearsal process is that a balance has to be struck between the Spontaneous and the Consciously Induced. Unlimited spontaneity produces slack, unfocused, self-indulgent results. Remorseless, conscious induction produces work that is stiff, artificial, and mechanistic. Ideally, the actor, like blind Gloucester in *King Lear*, must be brought to a plateau by his devious son Edgar, seduced by evocative imagery, and then left to jump. When Gloucester leaps from the great height of that "dread summit," he fully believes he is plunging to his death and, *because* he believes it, faithfully performs the fateful act. It is Edgar's directorial stratagem that persuades Gloucester both to commit his life and to save it. It is Gloucester's belief in the untrue and Edgar's faith in the value of illusion that bring about the old man's salvation, and it parallels almost exactly the actor-director relationship.

It is the actor's commitment to the director's vision that puts *his* life on the line and, likewise, saves it. Rescued from what should have been an inevitable death, Gloucester believes he has been traduced by a fiend. During the collaborative process, the actor sees the director in much the same light. But of course, Edgar loves Gloucester, and beneath all his stratagems, the director loves the actor, for it is only through the actor's genius that the director's ingenuity can flourish. "Set me where you stand," says blind Gloucester to the unrecognized son who will restore his faith in life. It could well be the credo of every actor on the first day of rehearsal.

7

Dialogue with Robert Lewis

Of all the original stalwarts of the Group Theatre—Harold Clurman, Lee Strasberg, Cheryl Crawford, Elia Kazan, Clifford Odets, etc.—the most unorthodox was the director Robert Lewis. While everyone else was following the aesthetic party line—which in the thirties was the Stanislavsky System, soon to become under Lee Strasberg "the Method"—Lewis was experimenting with a variety of nonnaturalistic styles, broad theatricality, and other preoccupations that did not endear him to the Group rank and file. As he explains in this dialogue, he was dubbed "Trotsky" for being something of a revisionist, but unlike his namesake, he did not leave the fold to create an alternative methodology. Instead, he extended Stanislavsky's teachings and directed some of the finest productions of the thirties, forties, and fifties—which include the hallmark Group Theatre production of Saroyan's *My Heart's in the Highlands*, John Patrick's *Teahouse of the August Moon*, Lerner and Loewe's *Brigadoon*, and a score of others. He became head of the Yale Theatre Department under Robert Brustein and is now active in Los Angeles, both teaching and directing.

Whenever I read histories of the Group, I always cheered silently that there was a Bobby Lewis in their midst. I felt him to be a kindred spirit long before I ever met him, for I sensed that, though bred in the gutter of thirties kitchen-sink realism, he, like Wilde, was looking up at the stars. He is, in my opinion, the only man of the thirties who has effectively made it into the eighties, the only director of that period whose aesthetic managed to keep pace with the changing times. Among his many gifts is an impish sense of humor, which makes it dangerous to turn one's back on him. The barbs with which he wounds one's common enemies can just as readily be turned upon his friends—although in Lewis's case, their humor would quite atone for their malice.

In writing about acting and directing, I felt it would add a different perspective to this book to include a dialogue with Lewis about our common concerns. What follows is an edited verbatim transcript of a conversation conducted in Los Angeles in April 1985.

MAROWITZ:

For a lot of people of my generation the legacy of the Group Theatre is a theatre glutted with psychology and naturalism; room-sized dramas and authors whose works are only a few notches up from soap opera. A theatre which discourages the creation of writers such as Beckett, Ionesco, or Genet and glories in the proliferation of playwrights such as Albee, Rabe, Mamet, and Neil Simon. A theatre, in a word, fixated at the level of the thirties, and one which does not reflect the dynamic currents of late-twentieth-century experience. Is this a fair assessment?

LEWIS:

I suppose you could say it's fair. What they said in the thirties was, we are going to have a theatre that reflects "the life of our times," and so naturally, they did plays by new and contemporary playwrights. Why they couldn't take classical plays or revivals and make *them* reflect "the life of our times," I'll never know! Well, no, I *do* know, and I'm going to tell you. The reason they didn't was that the directors of the Group—Harold Clurman and Lee Strasberg, who directed all of the plays—well, Cheryl Crawford directed a couple, but they don't count—they themselves were psychologically oriented. They weren't interested in language. They weren't interested in movement. They were interested in psychology. They wanted to do plays where people's feelings and relationships were important, and that's why they did those plays. Even when the Group tried to do something classical in 1939 that you would think would be very appropriate, namely, *The Three Sisters*, they couldn't get anywhere with it, and it was never produced. All the "means of expression"—that is, the way characters speak, the way characters move, the way characters dress, and so on, the behavioral things—they paid no attention to at all. All they were interested in was "true feeling." Their definition of truth, which was the basic thing at the Group Theatre and subsequently at the Actors' Studio, was a very limiting definition, because what they meant was the truth of *their* feeling. As a matter of fact, I remember we were told the question you were always to ask yourself was: "What would I do if I were in that situation?"—which is a lot of shit because *I'm* not Hamlet, *I'm* not Macbeth, *I'm* not Hedda Gabler. What you have to ask yourself is: "What would I do if I were *that* character, in *that* play, in *that* period, *that* class," etc. And then you use your sense of truth to transform yourself into that character. People in those days never played more than five minutes away from their own daily behavior.

MAROWITZ:

One has no great complaint against the Group Theatre and the social-realistic work that came out of it, because, as you rightly say, it was a theatre that reflected its time. But we're now living in the eighties and the legacy of the Group appears to be naturalistic writing and naturalistic acting. Does that put a poor construction on the Group Theatre as an influence?

LEWIS:

No, I don't think so. I mean, people have gone on from Freud—that doesn't mean Freud was a stinker. In his time, those were the things that people believed. Now people have developed further. In its day, the Group was a departure from the star system that prevailed at the time.

MAROWITZ:

But isn't it curious that just a little bit earlier at the Moscow Art Theatre, which also concentrated on social, realistic, psychological theatre, the offsprings of that movement were Meyerhold, Vakhtangov, Tairov—that's to say, a theatre in which there was symbolism, epic styles, classics, and theatricality of all sorts? One constantly thinks of the Group Theatre in terms of Method-ology, but as soon as you compare it to the mother company, which was the Moscow Arts, you see a very different kind of influence and one which was extremely diverse.

LEWIS:

I felt that all the time, I must say, and it was that kind of thinking that brought about my production of *My Heart's in the Highlands*, which was anything but realistic.

MAROWITZ:

Yes, you were actually the only one to swim against that tide.

LEWIS:

They called me "Trotsky," which was the worst thing you could call anybody in those days.

MAROWITZ:

What did they mean by that?

LEWIS:

Well, if you were a Stalinist, you see, Trotsky was a revisionist, and so they constantly called me "Trotsky." I remember very well in *Paradise Lost*, for example, which was a play by Clifford Odets, I played a firebug—a man who for a fee will set your factory on fire so that you get the insurance money. First of all, I reddened my hair, then combed it upwards so it looked like flames, and I wore a little black thing on my finger as though I'd burnt myself; I used a very strange kind of speech that I made up myself, and the whole thing was highly theatrical. And I remember when I started to work on the part in this way, one of the actresses in the company said [*disgustedly*]: "Is he going to start all that stuff again?" In other words, they felt that if someone was trying to find visualizations, theatricalizations of the insides of their character, that was wrong.

MAROWITZ:

Which, of course, is exactly the same kind of revisionism Meyerhold was accused of when he left Stanislavsky.

LEWIS:

Absolutely.

MAROWITZ:

It seems to me, the Method has crippled more actors than it ever helped, precisely by instilling the idea you just referred to—that the parameters of character are identical to those of the actor. It encourages actors to take epic characters and cut them down to dimensions they can personally handle. Is this one of the things for which we must really indict the Method?

LEWIS:

You have to indict all of the people who put into practice only one portion of it. Because, after all, Stanislavsky did all kinds of plays. He did Shakespeare, Molière; he even did Gilbert and Sullivan, you know. He tried everything. But they got stuck in the thirties. I remember Harold Clurman when he was dying, one of the things that worried him most was that people would think that the Actors' Studio was just stuck in the thirties—because you know, they're still doing their emotional memories and private moments and sense memory and all the rest of that stuff, and here we are in the eighties, a half-century later. Harold felt that Lee Strasberg had "ghettoized" the American actor. That was Harold's own word. That they never got beyond those early stages. When they do Shakespeare at the Studio, for example, what they do is take Richard III and bring him to themselves. I said to one of those actors once: "Did you ever think of taking yourself to Richard III?"

MAROWITZ:

It could be a very long trip for some of them.

LEWIS:

Yes, a *very* long trip. You see, they can't do it because they don't know how to speak or how to move. Their training has been limited only to emotional memory and things like that—training that ignores the means of expression, and that's why I parted from them long ago. When I became chairman of the Acting Department at the Yale School of Drama, I tried to deal precisely with that problem. In conventional training particularly on the East Coast, if you send somebody to voice and speech teachers or to movement teachers, they may improve your voice, give you a little more resonance, a little more range, whatever. But when you have a scene where Hamlet is going after his mother, for example, the Closet Scene, actors revert immediately to their old New Yorky way of talking. I had an actor working on that very scene in a workshop situation, and I had to keep correcting him. Finally, he turned to me and said: "What do you want me to do, talk or act?" As though there is some difference between the two. So what I did was the following: I brought the movement teacher and the voice and speech teachers into the rehearsals with me— so they could actually deal with the technical problems as they were happening, not in isolation from the work itself.

MAROWITZ:

That's a very legitimate thing to do in a school, in a learning situation, but are you suggesting there ought to be technical instruction in conjunction with directors during actual rehearsals?

LEWIS:

You bet your ass I am. Because when you get them in a performance situation, they lose it—all the beautiful voice and speech and movement things they got in those other classes. If they work on technical things at the same time as they are working on their parts, at least they come to understand that these things belong together.

MAROWITZ:

Harold Clurman used to talk about the Method as being synonymous with acting grammar. It was neither good nor bad, but simply necessary in creating a role. Is that too sweeping a generalization? Is there a body of technique and training which exists as an alternative to the Stanislavsky system and its derivatives?

LEWIS:

I don't think anybody has really taught the Stanislavsky System in its entirety—because if you look at the chart that Stella Adler brought back in 1934 from Stanislavsky himself, you will see that one-half of it has to do with the means of expression—right down to punctuation, movement, plastique, fencing, etc. All of these things are in the Stanislavsky System but not observed in any of the Stanislavsky schools.

MAROWITZ:

Are you saying that if the Stanislavsky System were applied comprehensively—in all its facets—it would be an all-embracing system? There would be no need for any alternative?

LEWIS:

No, because that man is dead, and that man died in 1938 or something, and life has gone on since. We should not undo the basic Stanislavsky teaching, we have to go on from there, because the theatre has changed, and so has the world.

MAROWITZ:

This leads me directly to my next question. The Method intelligently applied enables actors to uncover psychological subtext; that is, the stew of living meaning directly underneath the text. But is that the end of the line? Are there meanings and pertinences in a play that nestle below psychological subtexts, and if there are, how can the actor find these out?

LEWIS:

That's where the means of expression comes in. There's not only what one does or why one does it, there's also how one does it.

MAROWITZ:

Is there something beneath psychology?

LEWIS:

There's something beyond it.

MAROWITZ:

What is that?

LEWIS:

Not only what one thinks or feels but the behavior that emanates from your character.

MAROWITZ:

But that's also psychological, isn't it? Behavior corresponds to psychological states.

LEWIS:

It has to do with all sorts of things. It has to do with costume, with language, not only psychology. That's exactly my point. You cannot stop at psychology.

MAROWITZ:

Would you say the Method does not apply in the works of writers such as Beckett, Ionesco, or Genet?

LEWIS:

No, it's basic. It's like asking, "Is there any music where you don't have to practice scales?" You have to practice your scales in order to play the piano. That doesn't mean that all you have to play is Mozart sonatas. You can play Schoenberg; you can play Stockhausen. You can play everything, but you can't play *anything* if you can't play the piano.

MAROWITZ:

Therefore, in your view, the Method is a kind of basic grammar—the means by which you form the more complicated sentences of the modern theatre?

LEWIS:

I think it is basic to having a sense of truthful communication on the stage. To be able to speak and listen and feel yourself within the truth of a situation. That's what it's all about. Now, there are all kinds of situations. If they are realistic situations, then fine, you're home free. But the theatre is not always limited to that. Therefore, if you have problems with language, abstruse language, poetic language, rhythmic language, movement that is more than just lighting cigarettes and drinking wine but has to do with physical transformation of character, then you have to work to achieve that. I don't mean it must be done *only* physically. You always have to find some kind of inner justification for doing it—which in a way brings us back to our old friend Stanislavsky—because, after all, our behavior does not come just from the outside, but from the inside.

MAROWITZ:

I find that there are a lot of actors, and often they are very good actors, who are incapable of responding to theory of any kind—whether it's Stanislavsky or Strasberg or anyone else. What happens when you're dealing with an actor who operates simply on an instinctive level? In such a case, should one simply abandon theory?

LEWIS:

Not if you're a good director. If you're a good director, you can work with all kinds of people. Every actor that you come upon, Charles, is different. I've almost never found two actors who have the same problem. Somebody like Maureen Stapleton, for example, is a kind of "true believer," you know. She just believes everything. I saw her with her little granddaughter, playing with a toy telephone to show her how to use it, and she did it so beautifully I really thought there was somebody on the other end of the line. I mean, she just doesn't know how *not* to believe in something. It's part of her nature; it's the way she is; and that is her particular talent. However, she cannot talk, move, or do anything that is more than a short distance away from her own behavior pattern. I couldn't even get her to do Mrs. Alving in *Ghosts*. She says: "Oh, I can't talk like *those* people." I said, "What do you mean? It's not poetry, it's prose, and Mrs. Alving is no ancient relic. She's a very modern woman."

MAROWITZ:

Have you ever come across really good dumb actors?

LEWIS:

Really good dumb actors? How much time do you have? I don't know quite what you mean by "dumb." There are some people who cannot explain things in words, but somehow they hit it right every time. For example, there was a Sicilian actor by the name of Grasso, Giovanni Grasso, and he couldn't write his name. When he had to sign the payroll, he just made a big X. But he had deep feelings about life and relationships that made him a very powerful actor. Now, probably he couldn't do certain intellectual kinds of parts, I'm sure. He did Italian melodramas, but he was great in his field. There isn't only one kind of actor.

MAROWITZ:

Strasberg put a very strong emphasis on emotional recall, asking the actor to draw on his personal experience in order to find parallels with the emotions he or she was required to express. But Stanislavsky, as you probably know, virtually abandoned emotional memory in the last years of his life and put his emphasis on playing the objective on the very sound assumption that once an actor was engrossed in his action, true feeling would come about as a matter of course. Do you believe that appropriate emotional activity can be, as it were, researched in the actor in isolation from the scene that he's playing? Isn't the relevant emotional reaction precisely what every talented actor instinctively produces as a result of imaginatively accepting the fictitious circumstances of his role?

LEWIS:

If you have automatic emotional references, that's fine. In other words, if something is happening in your part and you understand it because in your own experience you have either lived through it or read about it and therefore have an automatic emotional reference for it, you don't have to do anything. You'd be a fool to say, "Well, I'm going to do an emotional memory here." There are times, however, when you need to look for something because you don't quite have it—except maybe intellectually. You understand the point, but you don't truly understand the experience. Then you have to go home and think about it and ask yourself a couple of simple questions. You don't have to go into all that digging that we used to do in the Group days; the old emotional-memory exercises. If you ask yourself: "How much do I understand about this; what is the nature of it really?" you will come up with something. Maybe not exactly the thing you're looking for, but something like it, and suddenly, it will kind of warm you up. As Ellen Terry used to say, "I need something 'to warm me up.' " She sure believed in it.

MAROWITZ:

But can it be researched in isolation? We've all heard of that classical Method situation where an actor has to find the right kind of emotional response for the death of his father and so is encouraged to think of his dog Rover that was run over when he was a child. Is it conceivable that emotions can be transmitted directly into the experience of a character from a wholly unrelated situation?

LEWIS:

Of course, because what you're dealing with is imagination. That is one of the biggest tools of an artist is imagination. You don't have to have murdered somebody to play Othello, for God sakes, but you understand in your imagination what it must be like because you understand how many times you've *wanted* to kill somebody, or how many times you've *actually* killed somebody with a word or with a look.

MAROWITZ:

Directors talk a lot about "directorial conception," implying they always seem to be proceeding from some kind of master plan. Do you always begin work with a clear-cut conception, or do you sometimes evolve one as you go along?

LEWIS:

I'm going to tell you a story about a director whom you may know called Ron Daniels. Do you know Ron?

MAROWITZ:

I know him, yes.

LEWIS:

I think he was originally South American, then he worked in England, and then he arrived at the Yale Repertory Theatre and did a production of *Bingo* by Edward Bond. Alvin Epstein played Shakespeare, and it was a lovely production. After the opening, we had our meeting with Brustein, who was the dean, chairing the session, and the first question that Brustein asked Ron Daniels was: "What was your concept?" And Ron thought for a minute or two, and then he said the following: "Well, I thought what I'd do was do the first scene as well as I could, and then I would go on and do the second scene as well as I could, and the next one and then the next, and when all those were added up, that would be my concept." Some composer once said to Shostakovich, "I can't find a theme for my second movement," and he said: "You shouldn't be thinking about the theme, you should just write the second movement!" In other words, just as in acting, these things that we're talking about come out of doing it, so is it equally true to directing. Now mind you, unconsciously every artist has a concept. It's almost the definition of an artist, isn't it? I mean, he sees something; he feels something about some material—whether it's a painting or a piece of music or whatever, and he starts to work. But the good artist, I think, solves the problems in writing the book, composing the symphony, painting the picture, or whatever. Now, in the back of his head, if he is an artist, he is being subconsciously guided by something that he sees there. Jackson Pollock is throwing paint along that canvas. Now, if that's all there was to it, we'd all be millionaires, because I can throw paint, too. There must be something different about the way Jackson Pollock throws the paint. He sees or feels something about that canvas and those colors, and when he's finished, there's a painting. He may not have started out with anything at all in his mind.

MAROWITZ:

But Jackson Pollock is working, in a sense, with himself, with his own talent. A director is working with other artists, who might be providing alternative conceptions of their own. We are often in situations where an actor comes to a role with preconceptions of what he wants to do, and in those cases, unless a director is actually honing his own interpretation, what is to prevent the actor from usurping his ideas?

LEWIS:

The cleverness of the way the director talks to him. If a director says: "That stinks! You do what I say!" of course it's going to be terrible, because even if the actor does it, he's going to do it in such a way you're going to be sorry you asked him. Part of being a director is being a psychologist and knowing how to deal with people. You have somehow to manipulate him and guide him to get him to fit into the larger idea. Otherwise, you're going to have a mess. And the better each person's different idea is, the worse it's going to be.

MAROWITZ:

Which implies that there *is* a conception on your part as the director.

LEWIS:

Right.

MAROWITZ:

Now, to go back to my original question: Can you really rehearse the play successfully without some kind of basic conception of your own? And if, as you say, there always is a conception even if you can't articulate it, does that conception automatically harmonize with other people's conceptions? In the case of Ron Daniels, could it not be, when he says he's going to do a scene as well as he possibly can, that he is simply encouraging the actor to produce the best results he can whether they pertain to his conception or not?

LEWIS:

No, because he's not a fool. He knows perfectly well that if he sees an actor is off on a tangent which is going to work against him, he throws out a suggestion to bring him back. It's a question as to how to say it. As I say, you can be a tyrannical director and make everybody do just what you want to fulfill your concept, and, I don't know, you might be able to make it work, but I doubt it. Because even Meyerhold, you see. . . . Let me tell you something about Meyerhold. We tend to think that biomechanics and all of that stuff was absolutely rigid and that he was a very inflexible kind of director. Now, some time ago, I saw the thing

Mel Gordon did, *The Magnificent Cuckold*. He tried to reproduce the Meyerhold version of it from photographs and writings and so on. And when it was presented, there happened to be a woman there; a woman with a long Russian name who was in her eighties or maybe even in her nineties. She'd been in the 1922 production of *The Magnificent Cuckold* under Meyerhold. Now, this young American cast reproduced this thing, and it looked quite interesting but quite mechanical. You know, everyone was doing their rhythmic movements, and so on. Anyway, when I met this Russian lady later that evening, she recalled what they really did. She described Il'insky, who was the leading actor, and she described Meyerhold, and she said it wasn't like that at all. The way she described Meyerhold's work, it was no different from the way any good director worked. There was no kind of arbitrary choreography and all that stuff. He just found new things as he went along—the way any good director does.

MAROWITZ:

But the fact remains that Meyerhold certainly was an autocrat-director: someone who gave line readings, inflections, gestures, and explained exactly how he wanted things to happen. And my own feeling is that the greatest productions of the nineteenth and early twentieth centuries were the work of what we disparagingly call "autocrat-directors": the Meyerholds, the Reinhardts, the Vilars. Is there a case to be made for the autocrat-director as opposed to the genial democrat who seems to have taken his place today?

LEWIS:

Well, I must say that Nazimova told me that she left the Moscow Art Theatre because Stanislavsky was an autocrat. She wouldn't take the way he treated her. So it's not only the "theatricalist" ones but the so-called "realistic" ones that were that way. Of course, there has to be a leader. What you're asking is how can the orchestra play if there isn't someone giving the downbeat; how can there be choreography if there isn't someone laying down the movements?

MAROWITZ:

I'm asking something else, really. I'm thinking about the autocrat-director as somebody who has a very specific image of every moment that takes place on the stage; who uses the actor, molds the actor, in order to convey that preconceived image. As opposed to the director who says. . . .

LEWIS:

You're saying two different things. You're talking about "preconceived image," and then you said—very quickly, but I want to catch you up on it—"every moment." Now, you can have a preconceived image, which, of course, you do if you're an artist, but that doesn't mean that you do not find in rehearsals different ways to realize what you want. And sometimes, when you come to the end of a production, you may be surprised how far you've strayed from your original image. Somebody who says, "I know every single move and every single sound of this image, and I'm going to make these people into puppets," I think such a person is going to have a very odd production. I don't think any of these men that you mentioned were like that.

MAROWITZ:

But Meyerhold was accused of precisely that—of turning his actors into puppets. He had a score. He had a formulation of precisely what gestures they should make. He gave intonations. He was as close to a puppet master as any director has ever been. And yet he was inexhaustibly resourceful and produced some of the finest productions of the early twentieth century. Is it that we've reached a point now where our attitude about democracy recoils from the idea of an autocrat?

LEWIS:

I don't think democracy has any place in art, I'll tell you that right off the bat. Democracy is fine if you want to vote about clean toilets or pay or rehearsal hours and things like that. You can vote from morning till night, but nobody can vote anything artistic; that must come from the creative source. And in the theatre, the creative source for all departments—the acting, the text, the scenery, the costumes, the lighting, the make-up, the music, and so on—must have the same center, and that center is the director.

MAROWITZ:

So you *do* advocate autocracy?

LEWIS:

Let's say I advocate a benevolent autocracy. The reason I say that, and it has nothing to do with sentiment, is that if these other people, the designers, actors, and so on, are artists, you have to get them to feel they are using themselves and not just doing what you tell them.

MAROWITZ:

You mean you have to delude them into thinking that.

LEWIS:

Of course. I never say to an actor, "Come in here! Then walk over there!" I always say: "Don't you remember yesterday when you came in here and then walked over there . . ." and they say, "Oh yes, of course." You have to make them feel that it's theirs.

MAROWITZ:

Is that not simply applying child psychology to actors?

LEWIS:

Call it what you will. You have to deal with people. Now, there are all kinds of actors. There are some actors that have to be beaten into performances. They're just too damn lazy. There are others, if you beat them, they just clam up and can't do anything. There are no dogmas about this, Charles. You're trying to pin me down to giving one answer, and I'm never going to do that, because things change all the time. They change even in the course of a production. You have an idea that you think is absolutely marvelous, and then something happens in the course of the work that's much better, and so you switch a little. Sometimes, of course, you have to change an actor. You made a big mistake. You thought he was going to be perfect, and now it turns out he's *too* perfect, too much on the nose. It's a collective art. You have to deal with all departments. You even have to deal with producers, you should pardon the expression, and sometimes you even have to trick *them* into giving you what you need.

MAROWITZ:

So delusion, manipulation, the use of child psychology—all of these things are necessary directors' tools.

LEWIS:

Right.

MAROWITZ:

You actually saw the performances of actors such as Jeanne Eagels, Laurette Taylor, Dudley Digges, Walter Hampden, John Barrymore. . . .

LEWIS:
Right.

MAROWITZ:
What distinguished those actors from comparable actors of our present generation?

LEWIS:
First of all, they could speak English. That's the first thing. They all had voices. Remember in *Sunset Boulevard* Gloria Swanson says: "In those days, we had faces." Well, in those days, we had voices. All the people you mentioned—I remember Jeanne Eagels's voice very well. Laurette Taylor, I remember *her* voice very well. John Barrymore, certainly. Walter Hampden made a kind of nine-teenth-century Shakespearean sound. Each one of them had a distinctive voice. Then Strasberg came along and said, "All of that is shit, you know, the only thing that is important is emotion, is 'true feeling.' " That was the collapse of theatre in this country, and I think it's going to take us a long time to get over it. It's perfectly true that an actor like Walter Hampden wasn't the great-est actor in the world, but a lot of these others were wonderful actors, and they were not just true to their own miserable psyches the way the Strasberg actors are. They played parts.

MAROWITZ:
Does it have anything to do with the fact that these actors were, in a sense, born and bred on the stage and not like contemporary actors, conditioned by media work?

LEWIS:
Absolutely. I go mad in my own workshop because people work all week with microphones. In films and television, you see, they don't want them to speak up. There's this little man sitting there with a knob who doesn't want the needle to flick past some point on his dial. If you get too loud, they just turn you down. If you're too soft, they turn you up. Also, film and television actors don't have to be able to think clearly the way good stage actors do. If they can't tell what you're thinking, they just zoom in on you and give the audience a close-up of the guy's eyes so that everyone can see that he is or isn't happy. The machine is doing all the acting for them.

MAROWITZ:

But is the difference between these great actors and the others we're dicussing only a matter of technique, more voice or more stage presence, or is there some other, some greater dimension which they had which contemporary actors do not have?

LEWIS:

They had theatrical personalities. They were not "the boy next door." I remember very well sitting in the balcony looking at these people—Jane Cowl and Bertha Kalisch and all of these actors— and I thought, "That's what I want," because it was larger than life. Then I got into the Group Theatre, and I was right back in my mother's kitchen again—which is exactly what I was trying to escape. There was real excitement in that theatre, even the way people made entrances. I nearly fell out of the balcony when they came on. Now we have a whole series of actors who work in films. Very few of them have tackled the great parts, and when they do, they just mangle them.

MAROWITZ:

They're smaller than life rather than larger than life.

LEWIS:

Right, but given the choice, I'd rather be larger than life.

MAROWITZ:

Does this have anything to do with the material? The plays that Jeanne Eagels and Walter Hampden and John Barrymore performed were very different from the room-sized, naturalistic drama that modern Method actors play. Could it have something to do with the fact that if you're playing *Cyrano* or a play like *The Jest*, you're encouraged to expand rather than contract?

LEWIS:

Of course. You see, it all goes together. We did plays that reflected the life of our times, as Harold Clurman said, and the style of acting went along with that. But now playwriting has changed. Plays have become fragmented like cubism. There's a little bit here and a little bit there. The whole business of introducing a character and developing it doesn't exist any more. There's no point in going back to that earlier time. We have to rearrange our training to suit our performance needs.

MAROWITZ:

There was a lot of classical acting in the 1900s and 1920s; a lot of Shakespeare, and, from all one can gather, it was very robust. Today, everyone seems to complain that Shakespeare is under-nourished; that the American actor lacks the skill and the expertise to play classics.

LEWIS:

We go from one bad thing to another. When, in the thirties, they said, "We've got to get away from all that!" they were referring to people like Sothern and Marlowe. If you listen to their records, you can hear quite clearly that they were really singers. [*Intoning musically*] "Romeo, Romeo, wherefore art thou Romeo." The last of that lot was, of course, Maurice Evans. But if you want to get rid of that kind of false acting, it doesn't mean you have to say: [*in a constricted Brooklyn accent*] "Romeuh, Romeuh, wherefore ar'dow Romeuh!" There must be something between those two choices. There's no reason why you cannot respect the language, have a feeling for movement, for period, and still be emotionally true—without falling into the Method slough. It doesn't help you at all if you have to do Lucky's speech in *Waiting for Godot* to throw yourself into an emotional memory. We have to retrain ourselves, and I've been fighting that battle—well, I won't say single-handedly, but I can't think of anybody else doing it at the moment.

MAROWITZ:

Is there an umbilical connection between the prevailing style of acting and the prevailing style of writing? If we had a different kind of actor in America, would it produce a different kind of playwriting?

LEWIS:

It's a bigger question than that, Charles. It has to do with our lifestyle outside of theater. It has to do with the fact that everything is sort of laid back now. It's the whole psychology of the country, and theatre, after all, is a barometer of the society. The problems we're talking about really have their roots in the way we live. I know people—Bing Crosby, for example, was a man I happened to know, and he was a very (I hate to use the word) cultured person. He was well-bred, intelligent, he could speak French, and so on, but he wouldn't let anybody know that because there's something not very macho about that. It's part of the "American thing," you know, to be a "regular guy." And if you speak well, people think you're a sissy.

MAROWITZ:

It's also part of the "American thing" to hide your light under a bushel—if you have intellectual inclinations to put them down, because to be "intellectual," in many circles, is synonymous with being pretentious.

LEWIS:

That's right. Don't you find it hard to find people to talk to? I was at a party last night, an anniversary party for one of my actresses. She's done a lot of television, and so there were a lot of TV actors around. I walked around that room and tried to find somebody to say something to. I literally couldn't find one person. They were all talking about the time they saw *Torch Song Trilogy*, or how great this or that TV show was, and about their agents and so on. And these are all people vaguely connected with the theatre, too, so you see, it's not only theatre practices that have made actors the way they are, it's their own lives that make them that way.

MAROWITZ:

I want to talk about rehearsal technique for a moment. I often feel when directing a play that it's a matter of tuning into the particular chemistry of the actors that I'm working with and the situation in which I find myself on *that particular day*; that if I try to premeditate what should happen in a given rehearsal situation, it doesn't always work out. Do you feel that each rehearsal day dictates what the work should be?

LEWIS:

I think you should prepare and then forget it. By the way, I think that also applies to acting. Wasn't it Pablo Casals who said you should practice the notes very carefully and then forget them? That's what an artist does. But as to specific activities on any specific rehearsal day, nobody can lay out a four- or five-week rehearsal schedule and say, "I'm going to do this, this, and this." You have to play it by ear. You have a general plan, of course, but you're dealing with human beings and with designers, and authors and actors, of course; each day has to be free and creative.

MAROWITZ:

How do you deal with inflammatory situations when suddenly everyone's nerves are on edge?

LEWIS:

Sometimes you get breakthroughs that way. That happens in class situations, as well. You have to take a risk. Of course, if you get too tough, you might lose them. I'll give you a specific instance. There's an actress who was very good in light comedy: Irene Dailey. She was the sister of Dan Dailey, who was a light comedian in the movies. Many years ago, Irene Dailey was in my class, and she always did drawing-room comedies, light parts, and she was very good in them. And I said to myself: "I think she's got more in her than that. She's covering up a lot." So I made her choose a scene—I don't remember now which one it was—where she'd be forced to expose herself and not just be charming. And she resisted it terribly, but I kept after her and kept after her, and finally, she broke down and started to cry. And I thought "Oh Jesus, she won't come back now." But she did come back, and do you know, after that experience, her whole acting career had changed. I saw it happen in front of my eyes on that day. She went from being, I don't want to say superficial, because the light things she did were very charming, but she changed her whole style and really deepened herself, and it made a big difference to the kind of roles she tackled after that.

MAROWITZ:

That solidification comes about, doesn't it, because very often actors accept other people's conception of who they are?

LEWIS:

Exactly.

MAROWITZ:

They get cast in certain roles and gradually assume this is their "type."

LEWIS:

Right. There are some very good actors in this country who are just too damn lazy to do anything other than what they can do easily. Also, as you mentioned, there is the pressure from agents and other people not to change. They say, "The public knows you as that, and that's what they want to see." I thought just at that moment of Katharine Hepburn, who is now quite different from the way she was when she started out. For years she talked a certain way, moved a certain way, because it was associated with her. It's only now that she's older that she's willing to play all sorts of characters and doesn't give a damn any more.

MAROWITZ:

In a lesser way, that was the case with Jack Lemmon, who also started out as a light comedian and has gradually taken on heavier and heavier roles. Now I want to ask you about the audition procedure. What do you look for in an audition?

LEWIS:

You can easily be fooled in auditions, I've found. Somebody gets up and does something they've prepared and rehearsed and maybe been coached in by somebody, and they do it very neatly, and you figure, that's good; they seem to know what they're doing. Then it turns out that's all that person can do. Somebody else comes out and they flubber and flounder around and are embarrassed and can't speak and so on, and yet you feel there's something there—if only you could get them over their fears. So you work with them. I tend to talk to them, to joke with them. I give them little problems to solve to get their mind going, and often, before the audition is over, you find that behind all that flubbering and floundering, there is a real actor.

MAROWITZ:

What is it you're looking for when you make those suggestions?

LEWIS:

It depends what you're auditioning for. If you're auditioning for a specific role in a play, as opposed to a class or workshop audition, you have to find out if the person has the basic characteristic of that part.

MAROWITZ:

And how do you find that?

LEWIS:

All sorts of ways. You learn a lot from interviews, as well as having them do scenes. If somebody has to have a lightness, for example, a sense of humor, and you talk to them and find they have absolutely no sense of humor, it's useless. There isn't anybody in the world who can "direct" you to have a sense of humor if you don't have one.

MAROWITZ:

Have you ever been deceived? I know that Strasberg was very often taken in by actors who were extremely intellectual, very cerebral.

LEWIS:

Also if they could cry. He loved that.

MAROWITZ:

Have you ever been in a situation where you were very taken by an actor's mind and then found when he got up on the stage there was no correlation between his ideas and his talent?

LEWIS:

Oh, sure, you can be fooled easily. You have always to bear in mind the essential factor of the part. That's the thing. Here's a corny example, but since it illustrates the point, I'll use it anyway. In the play *Rain*, there's this prostitute who, it turns out, according to Somerset Maugham, or John Colton, who made the adaptation, had more human qualities than the man of God, Reverend Davidson, who was actually a son of a bitch. Now, the important thing is not that the girl be able to play the prostitute well, because that's not the essential factor. (Actually the reverend is closer to the prostitute if you make the point of that play properly.) Now, when Jeanne Eagels played Sadie Thompson, she was the most innocent person in the world—despite the fact that she'd been fucking all those sailors. She was charming; she was loving and full of genuine feeling. Afterwards, everyone who played that role—Joan Crawford, Rita Hayworth, and on and on—were prostitutes from the start. The point of the play was never made. It was made, however, with Jeanne Eagels, because even though she did sleep around, there was something terribly human about her.

MAROWITZ:

She had somewhere to go as an actress.

LEWIS:

That's right. That's what you have to look for when you cast. Not where the character is, but where she's going.

MAROWITZ:

If you were going to give advice to a young man or young woman who decided they wanted to make directing their career, what would it be?

LEWIS:

Get together a group of actors who want to be with you and want to share your idea, whatever that idea is. But you have to have an idea. You can't just say, "I want to direct." There has to be some kind of underlying idea. It doesn't have to be theatrical necessarily. It could be a political idea. You could say, "I'm going to have a theatre that's going to glorify the working class," or "going to help South Africa," or whatever. Or it could be an idea that is purely artistic, that you want to do only classical plays or whatever. But whatever it is, once you have that idea, go and find the people who agree with you and want to work with you and are willing to sacrifice. (There's a nice old-fashioned word.) But you can't do without such an idea, because otherwise, the minute your actors get a job on radio or TV or the movies, they're gone. And that's why it's so hard to make a theatre in this country.

MAROWITZ:

Once you start work with this personal vision, as in fact you did in the thirties, does that vision stay with you all through your life, or does it get modified, diluted, sometimes even lost entirely?

LEWIS:

I should hope to God it would get modified. Who wants to stay fixed anywhere? But what should stay with you is that thing we had in the Group, of wanting to do it so badly that we went to any extreme to be able to do it. We didn't get paid very often. When we didn't have enough money to hire a secretary, we used to do all the envelopes ourselves, the mailing, the office work, every goddamn thing, to keep the thing going because we wanted it. It was our home, and when we did all those things it was like protecting our home. A proper theater *is* like a home, and a home is not the same as a motel or a flophouse. A home is permanent. You respect a home.

Differences of Opinion

8

A stage production represents the considered choices of the man or woman who directed it. Even those choices made by the author, the actors, and the designer are filtered and confirmed by the director, and so theoretically, everything on the stage has his stamp of approval. But in the final stages of a production—when the play is in runthrough or previews—those choices are fiercely scrutinized by a wide variety of observers, which include producers, agents, backers, and other "formidable persons" who feel the need to exert their opinion before the work becomes a finished product. It is at such times that the critical floodgates are opened and the whole question of taste—the director's and everyone else's—is energetically explored. It is at such times that the most "agonizing reappraisals" are made.

Every opinion, no matter how articulate or obtuse, is an expression of a person's aesthetic—even of those people who do not know what the word *aesthetic* means and who would stoutly deny having any such thing. Some people can analyze their reactions and precisely define their cause. Most people merely flounder for the first words that come to mind and convey only the fuzziest expressions of approval or dissatisfaction. And yet, at the tail end of a rehearsal process, when everyone is at his most vulnerable and hungry for evaluation, all of these reactions tend to be taken into account.

"Keeping one's head while all about you are losing theirs and blaming it on you" is a perfect description of the final stages of a troubled rehearsal period. Sticking to your own opinion is sometimes like clinging to a piece of driftwood that is the only thing between you and drowning. "Other people's opinions" can be like a descent of vultures—each of which fancies a different part of your anatomy. Sometimes the most courageous act in the world is to retain your own vision in the face of other people's persuasions; sometimes, of course, it's the most fatuous. It is difficult to shake off four or six or eight weeks of commitment to an idea that is not paying off, but sometimes, in those last crucial days before opening, precisely that kind of divestiture is what is required.

The real value of a conviction is that it proves itself during the rehearsal process—for you, if not for anyone else. But because rehearsals induce tunnel vision, it sometimes happens that a fresh set of eyes reveals the barren harvest of false premises. That is when a director, if he can leap the hedges of his own ego, shows his best mettle—the ability to abolish the regime he has lovingly constituted over many weeks of diligent labor, and hurriedly install a new order.

One of the most common courts of appeal in these last stages is "audience reaction"—a state of consciousness that each person interprets for himself. For the actor, the audience may seem to be tacitly approving his subtle choices. For the director, it may be squirming silently in an anguish of boredom. Virtually everyone will construct his own interpretation of the audience's reaction. The great truth about objectivity in the theatre is that, in the main, it is *subjectivity* writ large.

But does that mean there is no such thing as audience reaction? Surely that cannot be the case. We know that when audiences find something funny, they laugh. When they find something tedious, they fidget. When they are touched, they sometimes cry. When they are fascinated, they sit hypnotized. These are the self-evident manifestations of audience reaction, and, in most cases, they are indisputable.

But not every play seeks to elicit laughter or tears. In many dramas, it is the "hold of the play" that is of paramount importance—the play's ability to sustain interest in its changing patterns until its outcome is known. That is already more difficult to assess, for an audience's immobilized interest is essentially no different from its immobilized boredom. Many actors have encountered quiet, undemonstrative houses that sit "quiet as a mouse" and then, at the final curtain, explode with enthusiasm. Just as many have construed the still, regular breathing of rapt spectators as their being held spellbound, only to be greeted at the end by desultory applause and a swift, embarrassed flight to the exits. The actor's subjectivity, unless it is extraordinarily sensitive, tends to project its wishful thinking onto audiences.

The objective truth of an audience reaction not only is very different from what artists imagine, it also differs greatly from one audience member to another. To say that the "house" loudly approved of the performance simply because one-third of the viewers vehemently expressed their approval ignores the mixed or negative feelings of the other two-thirds, who may have had no inclination to express themselves one way or another. The same is also true of laughs. If half the audience erupts with laughter, that is not an audience reaction; that is *half* an audience reaction. The remaining half may be silently censuring not only the attempted comedy of the play but also the deplorable sense of humor of their fellow audience members.

Theatre, on both sides of the curtain, is an exercise of taste. Actors' "choices," directors' "interpretations," authors' "concepts," producers' "presentations" all confirm the presence of good or bad taste. Every conflict between an actor and a director is the result of one person's taste colliding with another's. And taste itself is a shorthand term for aesthetic values, moral sense, political bias, and philosophy of life. Every moral, psychic, and intellectual factor that breeds within an individual conditions that individual's way of inflecting a line, suggesting a move, designing a set, or producing a play.

Since the unbridled expression of all these viewpoints cannot possibly create a unity of effect, the theatre tries to find a way to harness the best of these impulses into some kind of common good. The harnessing is usually done by the director, and his taste is the aesthetic basin into which all tributaries flow. That's the theory, in any case. In reality, each collaborator in the process finds it difficult to relinquish his personal conception, and so rehearsals become subtle or overt struggles for power in which each person pits his taste against another's, creating, in most cases, a "working compromise," which is the production. The greater the compromise each collaborator has made, the flabbier the overall result. For the overriding truth about play production is that democratic process attenuates its workings, and the surest way to produce a catastrophe is unswervingly to honor the one-man one-vote principle.

Take some examples from recent history. Vsevolod Meyerhold

was, by general agreement, one of the most dictatorial directors who ever lived. During the twenties and thirties, he was criticized for converting actors into puppets, and manipulating them for the greater glory of his own ego. He even went so far as to create a technique, biomechanics, that would insure that actors could produce exactly the results he wished.

Once Meyerhold accepted a play for production, he sliced it up into segments and proceeded to reconstruct the work according to his own lights. Often, he wedged the work into a musical score of his own choosing—whether music was indicated or not. He insinuated his ideas of costume and setting onto his designers and refused any finished product that did not tally with his original conception. For some productions, he designed an entirely new stage using constructivist principles and forced plays intended for naturalistic settings onto rostrums, catwalks, treadmills, and raised platforms.

Meyerhold brooked no personal interpretation from his actors. Good performances were those that conformed exactly to what he wished to see on a stage; bad performances were those that diverged from the director's prototype. Frequently, he demonstrated precisely how he wanted a moment to be played, and the actor was obliged to imitate his movements and intonation precisely. He was the personification of the autocrat-director and demanded that every actor's individuality be subjugated to his theatrical command.

And yet, Meyerhold was indisputably one of the greatest directors of the twentieth century—for many, greater even than Stanislavsky, in whose theatre he started and who championed his earliest efforts. Apart from reenergizing the works of Gogol, Ostrovsky, Pushkin, Dumas, and Ibsen, he devised the "objective" theatricalist style of theatre that, by incorporating elements of the Living Newspaper, open staging, and topical political content, paved the way for Piscator's and Brecht's Epic Theatre. By insisting that psychological naturalism diminished the drama and that the theatre had to be involved with spectacle, metaphysics, and larger-than-life issues, he laid the groundwork for Antonin Artaud and his Theatre of Cruelty. By brilliantly integrating music, dance, acrobatics, and mime, he booted the room-sized, small-scale, petit-point naturalistic theatre into the twenty-first century. Happenings, multimedia events, Performance Art, and *verfremdung* can all be traced back to his theories, examples, or influence.

Stanislavsky, on the other hand, was a great believer in the actor's resources, and although he too could be dictatorial, his entire "system" was based on permitting the actor to tap the sources of his own inspiration. It could be argued that as a result of this approach, the actor developed his own potentialities and became a more independent and fully rounded artist, whereas Meyerhold's actors were largely ineffectual outside the framework of a Meyerhold mise-en-scène. But we must remember that Stanislavsky considered himself the handmaiden of the author, and his directorial efforts were always aimed at fulfilling the author's intentions. Meyerhold was his own author even when (*particularly* when) he produced the works of others.

In a sense, Stanislavsky, like a sympathetic foreman, could afford to allow actors to find and shape their own clay, for the "building of character" was part of a joint effort. His job was to see that the right "building materials" were used and the author's blueprint scrupulously followed. Meyerhold, like an action painter or a latter-day performance artist, was creating the experience as he went along, using the actors merely as components of his master plan. Stanislavsky had his form and content delivered to him by his playwrights and, on their instruction, assembled a squad of actors to realize their ends. Meyerhold was often delineating the theme of his production as he restructured a play's content, and so for him, actors had to be linked to the ideas *he* was concocting above and beyond the original material.

These are not only two ways of directing, but two quite different ways of viewing art. There is no contest between the interpretative artist and the originating artist. Each proceeds from a different premise. For the former, the actor is an equal partner in the creative process; for the latter, he is more an instrument of a premeditated design. The good actor should be able to insinuate himself when playing Ibsen or Chekhov according to Stanislavsky's approach, and to subjugate himself when playing Gogol or Dumas according to Meyerhold.

Of course, it rarely happened that way, and in the twenties and thirties, there developed two distinctive breeds of performer: the Moscow Arts actor, who was armed with his inner technique and his creative individuality, and the Meyerhold actor, who was often a brilliant pawn on the master's chessboard. Stanislavsky conjured up Chekhov and Gorky and, via Strasberg and the Group Theatre, the styles of psychological realism that paved the way for Arthur Miller and Tennessee Williams. Meyerhold invented a theatricalist approach that influenced the way we perform writers such as Ionesco, Genet, Beckett, and Brecht. But, as I say, it is not a competition. Just as Stanislavsky and Meyerhold were utterly complementary in their own time, so are the theatrical styles they spawned. In classical productions by companies such as the Royal Shakespeare, Le Théâtre du Soleil, and the Piccolo Theatre of Milan, they often march hand in hand.

The commanding presence of a superior artistic taste entirely justifies the subjugation of all others. In the theatre, it is always the superior idea that must hold sway, and that idea may emanate from the director, the writer, the producer, the tea girl, or the cleaning lady. (Unfortunately, these lovely democratic potentialities are overridden by the director, who, in most circumstances, must determine which *is* the superior idea.) It would seem to make sense to construct the mise-en-scène in such a way that, although firm in and of itself, it is still accessible to the revisions of last-minute inspirations and remedial thinking.

We must also recognize the fact that sometimes a dogmatic and arbitrary approach offers the best chance for a play's success, and that no democratically elected committee has ever succeeded in creating a work of art.

It is in those torturous last stages of a production that we should make a solemn pilgrimage back to our earliest intentions—either to reinforce the validity of the road traveled or to justify the new turning. The easiest thing to forget during the tumult of a rehearsal period is what it was that made us want to do a play in the first place, and what we hoped to accomplish with that tremulous matter that was so eagerly fingered in that far distant first reading.

And as for the tyranny of the "general consensus," all those contradictory opinions trying to assert their various wills, it must be constantly countered by the brute force of one man's personal conviction. We must regularly examine the temperament, values, and intelligence quotient of the people proffering advice. In almost every cabal of would-be and actual collaborators, the majority is made up of dunderheaded sots with opinions but no reasons, kibitzers without discretion, and dispensers of whimsical notions whisked out of the belfries of their personal idiosyncrasy.

It is a deplorable fact that for every talented artist in the theatre, there are a thousand gormless imbeciles, each of whom feels his "viewpoint" has the weight of a papal canon. Sometimes the only way to perform a creative act is by tucking your head into your shell and proceeding as if no one else in the world existed but yourself. Self-preservation and the cultivation of just such an arrogance often go hand in hand, and it is a union that should not be eschewed.

9

The In-House Critic

One night during a rather boozy London party, a colleague well in his cups smashed his drink against the fireplace and proceeded to revile me for writing drama criticism while simultaneously working as a theatre director. "Either you're in the kitchen or you're in the dining-room, goddammit, you can't have it both ways," ran the gist of his diatribe. Although I'd encountered the criticism many times before, it had never been put quite so forcibly or been made to feel like so heavy a malefaction. Throughout my professional career, the notion of a theatre practitioner's commenting publicly on the work of his professional colleagues was considered to be a lamentable breach of ethics. The ironclad assumption was that either one was a critic or one was an artist. If the twain did meet, woe betide the trespasser caught in the middle.

And yet, the greatest artists often have been critics as well. In poetry, Dryden, Pope, Wordsworth, Arnold, Poe, Yeats, Auden, Pound, and Eliot were equally efficacious as critics, and in the case of Arnold, Pound, and Eliot, exceptionally so. In French literature, Andre Gide is respected as much for his critical writings as he is for his novels—as are Paul Valery, the poet, and Francois Mauriac, the playwright. The complexity and discernment that Henry James reveals in his stories are just as visible in his critical pieces. Contemporary novelists such as John Updike and Anthony Burgess switch easily and eloquently from one genre to the other.

In the German theatre of the eighteenth and early nineteenth centuries, the two greatest dramatists—Gotthard Ephraim Lessing and Johann Wolfgang van Goethe—were also powerful critical forces. Lessing actually worked as a salaried critic for the newly established Hamburg National Theatre, and Goethe, who also acted and directed, became the first modern *intendant* when Duke Carl August asked him to take over the state theatre in Weimar. In France, Jacques Coupeau, who created the Theatre du Vieux Colombier (which spawned Charles Dullin's Atelier and the careers of Jouvet, Barrault, and Artaud), was initially and intrinsically a critic, and it was that critical spirit that shaped the aesthetic of his pioneering theatre work. In England, Harley Granville-Barker's writing on the theatre (particularly his prefaces on Shakespeare) is every bit as significant as his work as both a director and a playwright; and Shaw, who was a drama critic before he became a playwright, maintained his critical mien to the end of his life.

Closer to home, a man such as Harold Clurman, although essentially a director, spent many years contributing illuminating drama criticism to the pages of the *Nation* and the *New Republic*, and Robert Brustein, although primarily a critic, successfully combined his literary pursuits with the management of the Yale Repertory Theatre, as he does now with the American Repertory Theatre in Boston. The three most seminal influences in contemporary theatre—Stanislavsky, Brecht, and Artaud—were all critics of the institutions they inherited and gradually transformed. They not only wrote criticism, they also embodied critical attitudes in their professional work and dispensed highly charged aesthetic propaganda in order to change the status quo. There is no such thing as a work of art that is not fertilized by a critical spirit, just as there is no successful piece of critical writing that doesn't exemplify the precepts we associate with a work of art.

In my own case, theatre criticism was a great sublimation for my desire to direct in that period of my life when literary outlets presented themselves and productions did not. I started writing reviews at the age of seventeen for an incorrigible magazine called *International Theatre*, which appeared only twice; I joined *The Village Voice* in its earliest days to cover the then-burgeoning off-Broadway theatre and remained with the paper for fifteen years, dispatching notices on the London theatre scene. In the late fifties, I was part of the nucleus that founded the British publication *Encore Magazine*, which was rather noisily committed to the overthrow of Shaftesbury Avenue and the establishment of what it called somewhat fuzzily "vital theatre." Throughout the period when I was directing plays in the West End, in my own theatre the Open Space, and with the Royal Shakespeare Company, I was regularly reviewing my colleagues in the pages of the *New York Times*, the *Observer*, *Plays and Players Magazine*, and a dozen other British and American periodicals; and, I should add, being regularly reviewed myself in many of the same quarters.

Criticism and directing are, in many ways, two channels of the same energy flow. The director is the critic of the production, just as a critic, offering alternative approaches or speculation on roads not taken, often redirects the director. The rehearsal period itself is a time span during which self-criticism and objective criticism gambol hand-in-hand towards the opening night. The director, employing his critical faculties, is constantly refining the work of the playwright; the actor, overtly or tacitly, is criticizing the bevy of choices piled upon him by the director. The producers, designers, dramaturgs, and backers are regularly putting in their two cents' worth all down the line, and critical theories and propositions of immense complexity and far-reaching implication are being raised every moment an actor opens his mouth or decides to sit or rise. And yet, media critics remain the bêtes-noir of the theatre and, because they have such a direct economic impact on any given production, inspire antipathies between artists and themselves, which no amount of peaceful coexistence has been able to remove.

It strikes me that, over the years, the critic has been appropriated by the wrong institution. Ideally, he belongs to the theatrical establishment, and not the Fifth Estate. The media hire the critic to provide shopping tips or literary diversion, but to the extent that he delivers either or both, he is functioning merely as a journalist and not as a critic. Journalism, which sets great store by recommendations, dismissals, approvals, or disapprovals, is antithetical to criticism, which should be concerned with elucidation, analysis, and reasoned response.

Newspaper critics are obliged to deliver judgments, usually without having the space or intellectual acumen to marshal arguments. Like a bad actor who is prone to play results because he hasn't the craft to pursue the actions that produce those results, the newspaper critic spends his time rating rather than writing. He concerns himself only barely with that painstaking mental process that, when followed fastidiously, produces a coherent expression of the critic's feelings. The journalist is hell-bent towards generalization. The critic organizes his responses so that a generalization naturally evolves, and because it is the result of a progressive chain of reasoning, it loses all sense of verdict. It is the difference between a magistrate's perfunctory ruling at a traffic court with no time for nicety or mitigating circumstances, and the handing down of findings by a body such as the Supreme Court. The former is a hasty decision necessarily based on superficial evidence; the latter, a considered conclusion resulting from intensive scrutiny and extensive research. Of course, criticism always involves judgment, but newspaper critics, because of the pressure of deadlines and editorial injunctions to be snappy, readable, and topical, are almost always delivering snap judgments, and snap judgments are what make up the history of opening nights. That is nothing more than the *données* of the job.

The average critic is hurried, harassed, overworked, underpaid, an offspring of Grub Street rather than a child of Dionysos, and yet expected to deliver a conclusive appraisal that he must stick to no matter what second thoughts or conscionable *re*appraisals he might legitimately have the day after his copy appears in print. The rapidity with which most newspaper criticism has to be dispatched is lamented by both artists and critics, and yet the blast of an opening night followed by a next-day notice has become part of the glamor of the theatre, romanticized in Hollywood films and ritualized in places such as Sardi's where the morning papers breathlessly bring news of hits or flops. After all, runs the counter-argument, how long does an ordinary spectator have to make up *his* mind? He is forming his reaction as the evening progresses, and by the end of it knows more or less what he feels. Why should the reviewer, who is supposed to be merely a more articulate member of that audience, receive special dispensations to indulge in ruminations and afterthoughts that might never exist if time were not allowed to spawn them?

"When objects of any kind are first presented to the eye or imagination," wrote David Hume, the eighteenth-century Scots philosopher, in *The Standard of Taste*, "the sentiment which attends them is obscure and confused; and the mind is, in a great measure, incapable of pronouncing concerning their merits or defects. The taste cannot perceive the several excellencies of the performance, much less distinguish the particular character of each excellency, and ascertain its quality and degree. If it pronounce the whole in general to be beautiful or deformed, it is the utmost that can be expected; and even this judgement, a person so unpracticed will be apt to deliver with great hesitation and reserve." Unless, of course, he be a media critic who has learned to overcome his "hesitation" and "reserve" by striking that tone of Olympian assurance his readers and editors expect of him.

If indeed the critic is simply the average theatregoer writ large, there is no reason to grant him any special dispensations. If, however, the critic is a specialist with verifiable qualifications whose superior discernment is supposed to influence less sophisticated members of the public, the conditions placed upon his function should be different from those of the average theatregoer. But they are not. Both the media and the public expect him to deliver his critical goods with the punctuality of an overnight express service, and, huffingly, puffingly, his thoughts in disarray, his feelings flustered and his judgment glazed before his clay has been baked, he regularly obliges.

Consider the lot of this harried media critic alongside what I will now postulate as the In-House Critic.

Salaried by the repertory theatre or commercial management presenting an ad hoc production and concerned with only one show every six or eight weeks, the In-House Critic would be expected to write a review of the first runthrough, then the first dress rehearsal, then the first preview. Copies of these notices would be circulated to the members of the company, and in concert with actors, directors, designers, and playwright, his opinions would be meticulously examined. Once they had been assimilated, the director would decide which points were to be validated, which rejected. At best, the In-House Critic's reactions would produce beneficial change before the performance became public. At worst, they might force artists to reconsider decisions that weeks of rehearsals had solidified; but if that forestalled error or wrong turnings, would it be so terrible? It is, after all, the artist that has the most direct stake in the critic's perceptions, and in considering the artist's work before the event, the critic becomes a true partner in the creative process. He not only reveals what the artist has neglected but also assesses how much of his intention is actually getting through. The director, even more than the actor, needs the analytical power of the critic to confirm the implications of his work; to reflect how well or how badly the theme of a production is being expressed, *or* if it is being expressed at all. It is a great shame that Lessing, because of the resentment of the actors at the Hamburg Theatre, was persuaded to stop reviewing the productions of his own company, for if a critic is ever truly useful, it is in responding to the work of his fellow artists within the very context in which that work is unfolding.

In-house criticism need not be compromising or palliative. It should be as brash, candid, and impartial as it would be if it appeared in an independent theatre magazine. But what it must be is account-able, and being directed to practitioners who are encouraged to an-swer back, it would be. Criticism that is regularly obliged to justify itself develops better critics. The writing may still be suffused with ego and egocentricity, personal conviction, and personal idiosyncrasy, like the best media criticism, but what it will not be is cavalier, trivial, ostentatious, or grandstanding. The priorities of the media critic—readability, accessibility, conciseness, humor—are qualities to be found in all good theatre criticism; therefore, we should not create a false polarity between in-house criticism (assuming pedantry, verbosity, profondeur, and prolixity) and media criticism which is light, easily comprehensible, and to-the-point. The real difference is in grasp and background. Hopefully, the In-House Critic, because he is saturated in his subject and qualified to deal with it, would produce a more pertinent review—free of windy generalization, Olympian judgments, and cloaking glibness.

To a certain extent, the dramaturg or literary manager already performs the function of the In-House Critic, providing comments and reactions to directors and producers, and significantly, many of these posts are filled by former drama critics. (It is arguable that when Kenneth Tynan became literary manager of England's National The-atre, he exerted more influence on the British theatre in twelve months than he had in the full decade he spent as a critic. He not only affected the choice of the repertoire and encouraged the emerg-ence of writers such as Tom Stoppard and Trevor Griffiths, he also imbued the work of the company with a certain political flavor re-flected in the employment of directors and actors, many of them from the zealously committed Royal Court Theatre.) But the dramaturg is already closely wedded to the material being prepared, may even be responsible for its selection, and so is less impartial than the In-House Critic, who would not be brought into the proceedings until the show was in its final stages. And also, since the In-House Critic *is* a critic and exhorted to be critical, there is less conflict of interest than there might be in the case of a dramaturg or a literary manager who already has standing allegiances to playwrights and directors.

If a media critic is any good, he informs the artist, after the event, of certain flaws, omissions, or weaknesses contained in the performance. Had he rendered the same services before the performance was presented to the public, how much more sensible it would have been; how much more relevant to the work at hand. When a criticism is put to an actor or director at the runthrough stage, its validity can be immediately tested. If the actors and director disagree, they have an opportunity to challenge the criticism, and the critic is then obliged to explain or justify his position: something he is never asked to do in the public prints. Within the framework of a collaboration, the artist's attitude to the In-House Critic would be much more open and receptive. He would acknowledge that the motive of the critic is to improve and refine, not, as is so often the case with media critics, to vaunt his own ego or score points. That not only helps the artist, it also helps the critic. Defending his ideas in open debate sharpens his intellectual faculties and militates against self-complacency. The In-House Critic has a vested interest in producing the best result, and because his view directly condition that result, he feels himself a full partner in the creative process. As for the media critic (whom one is tempted to call the Out-House Critic), his loyalties are split between his readers and his editors, and he is little more than a parasite on the drama.

Fine, you will say, all of that may serve the artist, but what about the public for whom, theoretically, the artist is performing all these labors? Who is to advise *it* what to see and what to avoid? Who is to represent its uninitiated viewpoint? The viewpoint of spectators who haven't had the luxury of seeing the runthrough, the dress rehearsal, and the preview? What about the average customer who simply buys a ticket for a performance and, more often than not, wishes he hadn't? Or are we advocating a critic-free society in which public opinion is an irrelevance beside the artists' determination of their own worth?

The answer is, of course, that there must be two sets of critics: one for the artist and another for the public, but to avoid the current miasma (namely, journalists' disseminating half-digested reactions in half-baked prose to a largely indifferent public that doesn't trust them anyway), it is *critics* rather than *reviewers* that must be engendered, and the best breeding ground for these is the theatre itself. It is the In-House Critic who must eventually become the public drama critic; the man or woman whose sensibility has been refined by protracted exposure to the rehearsal process, the creation of character, the evaluation of mise-en-scène, and the translation of written word into performed action.

The media critic who arrives at his post after having been an In-House Critic is better suited to guide the public than the failed actor or writer, half-educated Oxbridge subscholar, self-styled armchair intellectual, or arbitrarily assigned newspaper hack who, more often than not, is the kind of person presently holding down the post of drama critic. When he switches from the theatre to the media, he acquires a new allegiance—i.e., to the public—which he will now discharge with an awareness and sophistication derived from direct contact with the living theatre. It will be much harder for artists to malign or dismiss the criticism of a man or woman who has actually been in the thick of the theatre and knows as much about it as they do—and hopefully, there would be no reason to. For the media critic will have gained the respect of those colleagues from whose ranks he has risen.

Once he has graduated from the playhouse into the public prints, the critic realizes that his tone of voice has to change. He can no longer employ an esoteric frame of reference or a specialized vocabulary. He has to make himself accessible to a general readership, but because his theatrical expertise will now be ingrained, he will have something pertinent to say and a more pressing reason to find the right words with which to say it. (He may even, given his new resources, be able to say it within the time strictures of newspaper deadlines.) Having served in the inner cabinet of the artists, he will be a much more creditable ambassador of the public.

The way to mend the breach that has existed for at least three hundred years between the critic and the artist is to recognize the symbiosis rather than the opposition between them. For criticism to be salutary, it must be tart, penetrating, concerned, and occasionally destructive. But if it is to be practical, it must be part of an ongoing interaction between criticism and creativity.

However, even as I write these words, I wonder, given the egos of the artists and the independence of critics, if such an entente can ever be reached? Can the commercial imperatives of the media, which are so far removed from the artistic needs of the theatre, ever be squared?

Probably, it is useless to generalize about criticism. The field is too variegated, the principles too elusive. All one can do is talk about critics—the good ones and the bad ones; the ones that epitomize those qualities of discernment and revelation one associates with a fine temperament and those who, lacking such a temperament, indulge in mindless advocacy or mindless denigration or simply tread water by spinning copy and, though they get nowhere, make a great splash while doing so.

Personally, I get a lot out of Stark Young, Eric Bentley, Harold Clurman, Kenneth Tynan, Irving Wardle, and Robert Brustein—almost as much as I do out of Dryden, Hazlitt, Arnold, Wilde, and Henry James. But in the case of most media critics, I feel there is an enormous gulf between what I do as a director and what they seem to be experiencing. As is often the case when one feels regularly misunderstood, I conclude: it is probably just me. We all live in different worlds, and a theatrical event is a pathetic attempt to invite representatives from all those cosmogonies to a kind of short-lived communal jamboree. Not everyone attends, and many that do find insurmountable communication barriers. As at all such gatherings, you make friends with a few and ignore the vast majority—as they do you.

What dogs drama criticism is the fact that no objective correlative has yet been devised that melds together the vast number of subjectivities that gather at a play. The best drama criticism unites the impressions of only a handful, and for every two who see eye to eye, there are twelve whose gazes never meet or who see a dog where you see an elephant or a mackerel where you see a swan. And yet, the critic proceeds as if the performance of a play were a common experience and reducible to shared perceptions. There can be no drama criticism without that premise. Whether or not it is a valid premise seems to me to be the most exigent question one can pose on the subject.

10

Adjusting the Classical Stance

A director's relationship to Shakespearean scholarship (Granville-Barker notwithstanding) is very different from an academic's. For the academic, theories, suppositions, and speculations are ends in themselves, and a really solid piece of Shakespearean criticism need only be well argued and well written to join the voluminous tomes of its predecessors. But a director is looking for what in the theatre are called "playable values"—that is, ideas that are capable of being translated into concrete dramatic terms.

Very often, scholars provide just that, and there is more "scholarship" on view in classical productions throughout Europe and America than audiences tend to realize. Most directors prefer to play down the fact that many an original theatrical insight is traceable back not to a director's leap of the imagination but to a scholar's dry-as-dust thesis. Two notable and acknowledged lifts immediately spring to mind: Olivier's Oedipal production of *Hamlet*, based on a psychological tract by Ernest Jones, and Peter Brook's *King Lear*, derived in large part from Jan Kott's essay in *Shakespheare, Our Contemporary*.

Although I have done a certain amount of reading and writing in what might be called "Shakespearean criticism," my excursions into that area have always been for practical purposes. When I approach a classic with an eye towards adapting, then staging, it, I tend to write myself "critical instructions" about the play, which may resemble "criticism" but are really more like Letters to the Director from the Adaptor.

These "letters" are clarifications for myself of what I feel about the play. They are highly subjective, quirky, usually indefensible in terms of Shakespearean scholarship, and occasionally perverse—in that they take into account only the ideas engendered in my own mind by the material, no matter how tangential or outlandish. In so doing, they often thwart or diverge radically from the play's original premise and its established literary meaning. They are a series of crackly communiqués received from the furthest outpost of the play's intimations, and I endeavor to incorporate their messages into the work I do.

Some of these communiqués are occasionally turned into coherent introductory remarks, as in the case of the *Hamlet* adaptation where I converted Shakespeare's material into a ninety-minute collage version, taking certain liberties with sequence, character, and theme. (See *The Marowitz Shakespeare*, Marion Boyars, 1978.) In this case, a reading of the free adaptation may clarify and, to the carpers, justify my remarks. In the case of *The Shrew*, I would likewise recommend a perusal of the adaptation, as it contains a great deal of original material not to be found in Shakespeare's *Taming of the Shrew*.

In the case of *Midsummer Night's Dream*, the text was presented more or less as Shakespeare wrote it, and I would hope my "notes" can be assimilated with whatever common knowledge of the play may exist. All that needs to be added here to clarify matters is that in the Danish production at the Odense Theatre in 1984, the play took place on a raked triangle of black fur, the traditional forest and fairies entirely banished. The role of Titania was played by a man in drag; Oberon was portrayed as a black-leathered field marshal à la Eric Von Stroheim in *The Grand Illusion*; Puck was played as an ancient, plodding, nasty old drone who moved very, very slowly; and the fairies were transformed into the kind of predatory homosexuals one encounters in the gay sections of many metropolitan cities. It is not my purpose here to discuss or dispute the productions themselves, only to reveal the kind of thinking that went on in the mind of the director before he set to work. The following notes are offered as examples of production fodder, not classical scholarship.

Introduction to Hamlet—Collage

No work of criticism that does not take into account the fact that *Hamlet* has been around for about four hundred years can begin to talk sense about what the play means to modern audiences. The critical canon is interminable, and almost every treatise on the play begins with a long- or short-winded apology for adding to a subject that, like love or God, has, through overelaboration, become permanently ambiguous.

Being neither a scholar nor a critic, I couldn't enter into that fray even if I wanted to. In fact, writing anything at all about *Hamlet* immediately induces a sense of playing the impostor, because a director, like a playwright, is supposed to say what he means in his work and leave speculation to that peculiar breed of niggling intellectual that actually enjoys picking at the chicken bones of art in order to recreate a semblance of the whole bird. So let me present my credentials from the outset—or rather my lack of them. I write as a director who, by dint of being one, must assemble and transmit the ideas he entertains about the material in his hands. The observations that follow are only rough indications of personal attitudes towards the play and the present reworking of it.

Five Questions and a Proposition

1. If we could see into Hamlet's mind, into the mind, that is, of a young man who returns home to find his father dead, his mother remarried, a ghost urging him to murder, a court full of treachery, a state threatened by invasion, and every imaginable pressure forcing him towards an act he is temperamentally incapable of, what would we see?

2. Is it possible to express our view of *Hamlet* without the crutch of narrative?

3. Is it not true that all of us know Hamlet, even those of us who have never read the play or seen it performed? Isn't there some smear of Hamlet somewhere in our collective unconscious that makes him familiar?

4. Can a play that is very well known be reconstructed and redistributed so as to make a new work of art? If *Hamlet* were a precious old vase that shattered into a thousand pieces, could we glue the pieces all together into a completely new shape and still retain the spirit of the original?

5. If Jan Kott is right and Shakespeare is our "contemporary," why can't we speak to him in our own tone of voice, in our own

rhythms, about our own concerns? Must we forever be *receiving* Shakespeare? Why can't Shakespeare *receive us*?

> I despise Hamlet.
> He is a slob,
> A talker, an analyzer, a rationalizer.
> Like the parlor liberal or the paralyzed intellectual, he can describe every facet of a problem, yet never pull his finger out.
> Is Hamlet a coward, as he himself suggests, or simply a *poseur*, a frustrated actor who *plays* the scholar, the courtier, and the soldier as an actor (a very bad actor) assumes a variety of different roles?
> And why does he keep saying everything twice?
> And how can someone talk so pretty in such a rotten country with the sort of work he's got cut out for him?
> You may think he's a sensitive, well-spoken fellow, but frankly, he gives me a pain in the ass.

The reactions that have grown up against both the psychological and historical schools of *Hamlet* criticism are completely understandable. Obviously, if you reduce *Hamlet* to a behavior pattern, poetry becomes irrelevant, and metaphysical elements are explained away by Freudian or Jungian tenets; and the only way to understand *Hamlet* entirely in terms of the Elizabethan sensibility is to be entirely an Elizabethan.

The great value of the Poel–Granville-Barker Elizabethan Revival was mainly technical. They discovered, quite rightly, that Shakespeare was being played too slowly, and that by playing him faster the plays made more sense and were more exciting. That is a simplification of a movement that had much more than that to recommend it, but that seems to me its chief practical value.

The view espoused by critics such as C. S. Lewis, that one better understands the nature of Hamlet by receiving the poem rather than analyzing the prince, ignores my very first point—that Hamlet, the prince, the character *as played by the actor before members of an audience*, has been around for about four hundred years. Our conception of Hamlet cannot help being eclectic. It is composed of first- and second-hand memories of actors such as Booth, Irving, Forbes-Robertson, Barrymore, Gielgud, Redgrave, and Olivier.

Every trait that any actor has ever emphasized in expressing his interpretation of the role is a hue in the multicolored image we have of the play. Every critical essay on the Dane has added complexion to that image. Where Lewis's argument falls down is that *Hamlet* is no longer the "Poem." The poem has been made flesh for us time and time again. *Hamlet* is a living amalgam of influences as dissimilar as those of the Elizabethan and the Victorian, the Freudian and the Artaudian. He is, quite literally, a mess: compounded of distortions, exaggerations, contradictions, all put through the strainer of time and delivered to a twentieth-century sensibility that is itself as complicated and contradictory as the long history the character has passed through.

That, for me, was the starting point. *Hamlet* the play, the structure that Shakespeare built and the sequence that Shakespeare assembled, had stopped *meaning*. We had almost stopped listening, in the way that we stop listening to an old and familiar tune after mechanically noting its strain and associations. But just as old tunes are continually being rearranged in modern settings, so it is possible to reshape, re-think, restress, and redress old plays.

And, of course, Shakespeare was doing so all the time. He was reworking and rehashing the commonplace narratives of his day; using Holinshed, Boccaccio, Surrey, Kyd, Marlowe, and the others for his own purpose; taking plays, or parts of plays, and giving them a treatment directly comparable to that which modern arrangers apply to folk songs and standards. Of course, the reworking in Shakespeare's case produced unique and original creations—a synthesis and perfection of all the elements that had preceded him.

But even perfection can pall with time, and *classic* can become nothing more than a hands-off label that critics and scholars affix to their favorite works in order to try and preserve the pleasure they originally received from them. When that happens, it is time for a "classic" to be declassicized.

Hamlet, after all, is a very special case. It is the most often performed, the most widely read, the most thoroughly studied of Shakespeare's plays. It has—quite literally—been done to death. It has become a myth, compounded of misunderstandings, distortions, and contradictions.

It is a man in black sprawled on a gravestone with a skull in his hands. It is a man looking fixedly at empty air. It is everyone who cannot make up his mind; who talks one way and behaves another.

It is the wilful son of a vain mother, and the misunderstood stepson of an unsympathetic stepfather. It is the angry young man flouting conventions, and the cool hipster tuned into Zen contemplation and eschewing violence. It is the LSD tripper floating free on his "expanded consciousness." It is the man caught between psychological uncertainties and moral necessities; the man who is provoked by politics and paralyzed by politics, terrified by the bomb and committed to the bomb; the man weighted with the knowledge that in a corrupt world, whether one acts honorably or not at all, harm is done and corruption grows.

All of these *pertinences* are in the play, but are not demonstrable because the play is imprisoned in its narrative. The play *is* the story, and to present "the play" is to retell the story. No matter what the interpretation, it must be expressed through the narrative line, through the progressive fiction of the play's given situations. And it is this relentless *narrativeness*, this impregnable closed circuit of storylines, that constricts the power and suggestiveness of what the play has become. Once the narrative sequence is broken, we have direct access to the play's ambiances. We rip open the golden lid of the treasure chest to find other riches within. After a rapid inventory, there is nothing to prevent us from closing the lid once more. A spliced-up *Hamlet* doesn't destroy the play forever, just as a beautiful woman who is raped isn't barred from future domestic felicity.

For me, the crucial question about Hamlet was not how mad or how sane, how reflective or how active? but is it possible, today, to sit through the play as Shakespeare wrote it and still respond to its story and structure? The play has become, like a well-worn violin concerto or an opera, a test for virtuosity—either the actor's or the director's. We wait to see what Actor X will do with the big soliloquies or Director Z with the battlement scenes. If the actor is an Olivier or the director a Guthrie, we usually get our money's worth. We are given something "different" and therefore stimulating, but are we being given the original artistic totality? Are we being moved or impressed by the fable as Shakespeare wrote it?

A good director or actor can, through original interpretation, reorganize the meaning of the play so as to give it unexpected relevance. When Orson Welles gives us a fascist-dress *Julius Caesar*, he is using sixteenth-century language in order to convey a twentieth-century attitude, and the compatibility of these two seemingly disparate elements captivates us. When Peter Brook gives us a bleak, remorseless *King Lear* unfolding in a world without God or purpose, he is using a Shakespearean text to convey a contemporary state of mind in a way that reinforces both the new conception and the old work.

We all snicker at eighteenth-century "improvements" that distorted Shakespeare's plays—even to the extent of reprieving doomed heroes and rewriting the poetry—but that was the age asking art to reflect it and balking when it did not. As an attitude, it is quite defensible. When Brook chops out the servant scenes after Gloucester's blinding, he is doing something very similar: not crass bowdlerization but deliberate editing in order to express a personalized view of the whole. The magical property of a masterpiece is that it can be made to *mean* again even when a society no longer thinks the way its author did at the time of writing.

Directors have been finding "new meanings" in the works of Shakespeare for centuries. No one questions any longer the director's right to reinterpret a classical work according to his own lights—to change its period, place a new emphasis on certain characters or relationships, or even, as Brecht did, rewrite plays in order to drive home one implicit idea at the expense of all others. It is this free and easy attitude to Shakespeare that has provided productions as remarkable as Guthrie's Ascot-dress *Troilus and Cressida*, Littlewood's First World War *Macbeth*, and Barton and Hall's amended and supplemented version of the Histories. But what has remained sacrosanct in Shakespeare is the language, the structure, and the narrative. One of the questions behind the present undertaking is to discover to what extent we can juggle *those* elements and still maintain contact with what is essential in *Hamlet*.

I do not contend that all of Shakespeare's plays are susceptible to the treatment that has been given here to *Hamlet*. As I say elsewhere, one of the prerequisites for Shakespearean collage is the audience's general familiarity with the play. In the case of *Hamlet*, we have the added advantage of a play with a mythic base that gives an audience an even wider, though less explicit, frame of reference. I think the same would apply in the cases of *Macbeth*, *Othello*, and possibly *King Lear*, and be quite inapplicable to the Comedies or Histories.

For centuries, the nobility of *Hamlet* the poem has been confused with the man himself. It is possible for a man to make eloquent speeches and still be a weakling and a coward, to have intellectual perceptions and moral insights and still be made of wax. Remove the romantic aura that surrounds Hamlet, the Renaissance prince, the man of heightened sensitivity, and look at him in cold blood, and the story of the play is quite different.

Hamlet, an aristocrat playboy who prefers amateur dramatics to ruling a kingdom, returns home after his father has died under mysterious circumstances. Now that the rightful heir is back, everyone expects him to deal with a situation that cries out for remedy. Knowing he is not equal to these expectations, Hamlet desperately tries to adopt an acceptable social stance. A ghostly visitation from his dead father confirms what he already suspected, but since it prods him into the kind of direct action he is incapable of, he decides to dispute the legitimacy of the apparition. Instinctively, he feigns madness. Madness is the conventional escape route for human problems. The madman is not expected to cope, and nobody blames him. But Hamlet's rationalization is that this cunning trick will make it easier to ascertain his stepfather's guilt, a contention he could never justify but that, fortunately, no one asks him to.

Incapable of real action, he sets about doing what he does best: preparing an amateur entertainment. Buoyed up by its success (the king's guilt confirmed), he encounters Claudius at prayer. Reality sobers up fantasy, and he realizes he is being given an opportunity to fulfill his father's command and still derive some honor from the deed. But he rationalizes yet another delay and, instead, decides to take on his mother, who is easier to handle. Being both a bungler and a hypocrite, he stabs the concealed Polonius, hoping he is the king but knowing full well that cannot be, since he just left the king at prayer.

With Gertrude as a captive audience, he proceeds to work off his actor's frustrations by playing the self-righteous son admonishing the adulterous woman. Once this pose is exhausted, he gets what he really came for: the maternal bosom and a good-night kiss. Having only the corpse of Polonius as a kind of third-rate symbol for the act he should have committed, he drags it off to show the world that even if he cannot revenge the death of his father, at least he can stab the vitals out of an officious old windbag hiding in ladies' closets.

Fortunately, the murder of Polonius compels Hamlet to be removed from Denmark, a decision he never disputes, since he is glad of any opportunity to make tracks. He rigs the murder of two old schoolfriends, not so much because they have become traitors but because, as with Polonius, the more he destroys the appendages of the king, the better he can rationalize the abrogation of the vow he made to his father.

Back in Denmark, no longer the subject of the people's expectations, a kind of aging playboy with all his credit gone, spurned by his own countrymen, Laertes foisted in his place, Hamlet is in the last stages of disrepute. Not only will he never be Fortinbras, he will never even be Laertes. His father's command is, by this time, a long-standing broken vow. His enmity towards the king has dwindled into pique. No one, least of all Hamlet, is taking it very seriously. The spectacle of Laertes's impassioned grief at Ophelia's funeral forcibly reminds Hamlet of the man he could have been. He quickly simulates a passion to show the world that there is still some fight in the old war-horse, but everyone recognizes that as just another histrionic display. Gertrude, no longer the subject of a moral quarrel but simply the "mum" of old, soothes her distracted baby.

The promise of a duel with Laertes before the court and in the presence of the king is Hamlet's pathetic comeback chance. Here, at least, he will be able to show his mettle: to suggest that *had he wanted to wreak a terrible revenge*, nothing could have stopped him. The duel, like the Play Scene, is a staged event, and so, naturally, he warms to it. To the end of his days, he will drone on to Horatio about "He that hath kill'd my King and whor'd my mother." In fact, had Hamlet lived to a ripe old age, he would have become as tedious as old Yorick must have been, describing the feats he *might have* performed; aggrandizing the misadventure of Polonius's death, his sly handling of Rosencrantz and Guildenstern, etc.: a pathetic old bore given to spiritualism and nostalgia for the "good old days" before the reign of Fortinbras.

In the Duel Scene, though he suspects foul play, he takes no precautions. He is almost like a man too weak for suicide, hoping some accident will dispatch him. Told he has been poisoned and has only minutes to live, he flares out all over the place, finally killing the king, but in such a mindless state of panic that the act is devoid of any honor or dignity. Horatio, the "good friend" who can be relied on not to reveal embarrassing truths, be they halitosis, body odor, or moral cowardice, lets the dying prince play out his final role: Death of a Hero. Desperately trying to contain a snigger, he hears Fortinbras order a soldier's funeral for this effete, aesthetic, intellectual non-starter.

As for Hamlet, in his last words the two main themes of his life combine: 1) his egoism requests that Horatio go about putting out a good review of his deplorable performance; and 2) he acknowledges his total inadequacy for ever having been ruler of the kingdom and says, virtually, "Thank God a real man is on the way; this rotten old country needs a leader, and I always knew it wasn't me—even though I couldn't say so." The rest is silence, just as the former had been cowardice, fantasy, and empty bombast.

Words and Actions

Hamlet, like many contemporary intellectuals, equates the taking of a position with the performance of an action. He is like those zealous paraplegics who fume about South Africa or the occupation of Afghanistan, and believe that the intensity of their convictions in some way affects the issue—that by trumpeting their moral righteousness to the world, they are actively remedying a situation. Compare such people with the less demonstrative activists who infiltrate black townships and get their heads bashed in, or risk their civilian lives supplying plasma and medicine to the wounded of Cambodia, or organize Latin American conspiracies under the constant threat of imprisonment, and the pseudoadventurousness of the "intellectual position" is woefully revealed.

Like these armchair commandos, Hamlet brilliantly defines his private and public dilemma: what has happened; what it portends; what must be done about it. The paralysis that ensues is delightful, because it enables him to indulge both his fantasy and his masochism. That is, he glories in having an important job to do and lashes himself for not being up to it. He feeds on the violence seething in his mind and asks for nothing more than its delicious implications.

It is very much like the situation of a man who derives more satisfaction from masturbation and erotic imagery than from intercourse with a real woman. After a time, no actual contact can compare with the delights of his own fancy. For Hamlet, the prospect of killing Claudius is too titillating to be obliterated by the physical act of murder, and he postpones that act the way the onanist draws out the actions leading to orgasm. Hamlet's murder of Claudius in the last scene is, compared to the speculations of "Now he is praying And now I'll do it" and the joyful discoveries after the Play Scene, utterly perfunctory. It is a delay that is not only dishonorable but also perverse. In fact, it is the perversity that makes it so dishonorable.

Fortinbras and Hamlet: Jekyll and Hyde

Fortinbras is Hamlet; Hamlet is Fortinbras: in everything, that is, but leadership, resolution, and action. When Hamlet refers to a "delicate and tender Prince whose spirit is with divine ambition puff'd," he could use no better words to describe himself. (It is curious that Hamlet and Fortinbras never perform on the stage together. Only when Fortinbras exits does Hamlet appear, and it is only after Hamlet is dead that Fortinbras arrives. The Jekyll-Hyde parallel is fanciful rather than provable, but it reinforces the theory that Fortinbras is a kind of wish fulfillment conjured up by Hamlet: a marvelously wrought figment who soldiers where Hamlet shirks and who reigns after Hamlet disappears.)

Hamlet needs Fortinbras: that is, a somewhat unreal and abstract figure to emulate and admire, because if he were to choose his models closer to home, he would have to fasten onto Laertes, and that would be too humiliating. It is all right to make a hero of an unfamiliar stranger, but if you acknowledge the same virtues in one of your own generation, you automatically disparage yourself. Laertes whores honestly, feels passionately, fights impulsively, and speaks directly. He has all the makings of kingship. Hamlet toys with women's affections, whores furtively, prefers internal struggles to open combats, would rather rationalize than actualize his passions, and is continually in doubt as to how much he honestly feels and how much he is dramatizing. A man of straw prefers imaginary heroes to superior versions of himself.

There is very little evidence to suggest that Fortinbras is the great man Hamlet makes him out to be. Fortinbras does not act boldly against the State of Denmark as his father did. He merely "pesters" Claudius with "messages importing the surrender of those lands lost by his father." When he actually arrives on the soil of Denmark, he is courteous and unbelligerent. He "craves the conveyance of a promis'd march over his kingdom." That is, he requests permission to move on to Poland—not for any significant battle, but to appropriate a little patch of ground "that hath in it no profit but the name."

This small-scale colonial adventure to gain a tiny sphere of influence is the act that Hamlet so aggrandizes in his next soliloquy, where he proclaims the dubious dictum: "Rightly to be great Is not to stir without great argument But greatly to find quarrel in a straw When honour's at the stake"—a justification all imperialist powers have used in appropriating territory that doesn't belong to them. But it is not the act that impresses Hamlet—he has neither the interest nor the political awareness to understand it (a lowly captain clues him in on all the details); it is the gesture that impresses him—a readiness to play the hero; make the grandstand play; act with conviction—no matter how wrong-headed it may be (the same sort of reasoning that decides Hector and his cohorts on the Trojan War). Hamlet is more susceptible to the stance and the show than he is to the personality and the true intentions. He sees a splendidly bedecked soldier cross the stage at the head of a large army. There is pomp, power, and all its glittering trappings. Here is a subject rife for identification.

The attempt to justify this watery Wittenberg intellectual as a "real soldier" stems from the confusions of the last scene. Horatio hits the right note when he uses feminine imagery in his eulogy to Hamlet: "Good night sweet Prince, and flights of Angels sing thee to thy rest." Flights of angels are really more appropriate than "four captains" and a military funeral.

It is Fortinbras, the soldier nonpareil, who trots out all the misleading military imagery; who calls for "the soldiers' music and the rites of war." He has just conquered in Poland; he is thick with combat; he has buried many of his own men in plundering a foreign country. A volley blast heralds his arrival at Elsinore. Not knowing the weakling the Prince of Denmark was, but seeing him in the midst of carnage, he assumes, quite wrongly, that Hamlet—like himself—was ever the man of action.

Had Fortinbras been around for the previous four acts, he would more likely command a patch be rooted out beside the dead Ophelia; that would really be a fitter resting place for the milk-water prince. But Fortinbras measures everyone by his own yardstick, and the dead Hamlet benefits from the miscalculation. It is just the sort of mistake a fatuous soldier, awed by royalty, would make. The cruelest sentiment in Fortinbras's last speech is "For he was likely, had he been put on, to have prov'd most royally." How was Fortinbras to know that in fact he *was* "put on" from his first encounter with the ghost to the duel with Laertes and, in fact, prov'd most unroyally?

Ophelia = Lolita

I cannot think of Ophelia except erotically. Despite her primness at court, her guarded attitude to the prince, her upright and officious father (what kind of mother did she have, I wonder?), there is still something palpably voluptuous about her. The very first time we see her, Laertes (himself so great a rake that his father must put watches on him when he travels abroad) is urging her not to open her "chaste treasures" to Hamlet's "unmaster'd importunity"—an exhortation that smacks of closing stable doors after the horse has fled.

Ophelia, a hipster beneath her courtly silks and laces, quite rightly shrugs off moralistic advice from a libertine whose "primrose path" is vividly imagined by Polonius (act 2, scene 1) leading to "such a house of sale, *Videlicet*, a brothel or so forth." Laertes, a well-connected youth at court—and therefore at leisure—has done his share of whoring, and his sister, confined to filial duties, has got all the backwash. More than likely, her appetites have been whetted: this ostensibly prim daughter of a leading court councilor, continually urged to chastity, in a society brimming over with promiscuity—a world teeming with forbidden delights.

Her situation is made even more delicate because the heir apparent has taken a fancy to her, and Father is in the government. Personal inclinations are at odds with political decorum in a state already made tense by a king's sudden death and the speedy and incestuous marriage of queen to king's brother. No sooner has Laertes told Ophelia to keep a watch on herself than her father picks up the same strain, and there is no mistaking Polonius's fear:

> Do not believe his vows, for they are brokers,
> Not of that dye which their investments show,
> But mere implorators of unholy suits,
> Breathing like sanctified and pious bawds,
> The better to beguile.

Polonius recognizes Hamlet's motives; so does Laertes, and it would be too great an insult to her female intuition to suggest that Ophelia does not. Another proof that Hamlet's intentions are strictly dishonorable is that hideous love poem that Polonius has probably browbeaten out of Ophelia, although he claims it was given him out of obedience. (Significantly, he claims it twice in quick succession.)

> To the Celestial, and my Soul's idol, the most beautiful Ophelia.
> Doubt thou, the stars are fire,
> Doubt that the Sun doth move,
> Doubt Truth to be a liar,
> But never doubt, I love.
> O dear Ophelia, I am ill at these numbers: I have not Art to reckon my groans; but that I love thee best, O most Best, believe it. Adieu.
> Thine everymore, most dear Lady, whilst this machine is to him,
>
> > Hamlet

It is precisely the sort of poem a man without real passion manufactures in order to make a woman more sexually accessible. And is there anything less characteristic of Hamlet than those stilted emotionless phrases?

Ophelia has certainly yielded to Hamlet before the play has begun. That is why, when she discovers her chances of marrying into royalty destroyed by Hamlet's unexpected aberrations, she feels "of ladies most deject and wretched," having "suck'd the honey of his music vows."

Immediately before this speech, Hamlet, raging with that feigned madness so temperamentally comfortable to psychotics that it has quite rightly created suspicions about his true sanity, has flung Ophelia's loose moral behavior back in her face. When Hamlet cries "Get thee to a nunnery" (i.e., whorehouse), his distaste is twofold: that he could sink to the same kind of lust with Ophelia as his mother is guilty of with his stepfather, and that Ophelia should be as accessible to him as Gertrude was to Claudius. It is the classic repulsion of the lover who despises his sexual object because he discovers she is just as readily enjoyed by others.

In this scene, Ophelia is the substitute for Gertrude. One scene later, Hamlet will be using his mother as a pretext to berate Ophelia. The sexual repugnance—essentially hypocritical but no less strong for being so—is perfectly consistent from the Nunnery Scene to the Closet Scene. Hamlet humiliates Ophelia, wanting to wound Gertrude: both are guilty (in his mind) of the same sin. In the Play Scene, he toys with Ophelia in order to disconcert his mother, and in the Closet Scene, after the emotional liberation of the play scene, he aims his hostility directly at its true object.

From then on, Ophelia, her usefulness ended, no longer figures in his life. Just before she dies (her repressions having already exploded into insanity), she acknowledges her promiscuity in the bawdy songs she may now sing quite openly. She is freed of the social inhibitions enforced by father, brother, and position at the court. Madness is her escape hatch. Quite likely, Hamlet did "promise her to wed" before "tumbling" her, but certainly it would never have come to pass had she "come to his bed" or not.

None of these observations is contradicted by Hamlet's passionate outburst at Ophelia's grave. Being a psychotic, he finds it easy to convert what was once a flighty deception into a passionately held belief. He "lov'd Ophelia," he bleats to the world; "forty thousand brothers Could not with all their quantity of love Make up my sum."

But essentially, the scene is a kind of irrational contest with Laertes: another son of a murdered father; another contender for the crown, and in almost every respect, a stronger contender than Hamlet. When Laertes's father is killed, Laertes moves swiftly to revenge. Returned to Denmark and sensing the teeming corruption of the state, he has already organized resistance, and a properly incensed mob is demanding: "Laertes shall be King."

In every comparable situation (and many of them are identical), Laertes does what Hamlet ought to. At Ophelia's funeral, Laertes quite naturally professes love for his dead sister. Hamlet, who cannot abide any passion that is stronger than his own theatricality, construes that as a challenge, and Laertes, the honestly mourning brother, is transformed into a rival, and—irony of ironies—a rival for one that Hamlet himself never loved. The gist of his hysterics at the grave is not really about Ophelia, but about his capacity to outdo Laertes in lamentation. Laertes's feelings are simple and direct:

> Lay her i' the earth,
> And from her fair and unpolluted flesh
> May violets spring.

Hamlet's are rhetorical and false:

> Be buried quick with her, and so will I:
> And if thou prate of mountains, let them throw

> Millions of acres on us; till our ground
> Singeing his pate against the burning zone
> Make Ossa like a wart. Nay, and thou'lt mouth,
> I'll rant as well as thou.

Returned from England, memories of the English tragedians fresh in his mind, the Lord Hamlet, a blustering phony to the end.

To say that Ophelia is like Lolita is at once a distortion and an extension of certain truths about the character as Shakespeare depicts her. To see her as a court dolly, a sexual convenience passed methodically from one nobleman to the other and even turning up in Claudius's bed, is, of course, untrue in terms of Shakespeare's text, but a conceivable fantasy in the mind of a man who, obsessed with images of lechery and incest, is prone to more hallucinations than Shakespeare himself might have imagined.

The Ghost

The perennial problem of the ghost is how to make awesome something modern audiences do not take seriously. The answer, traditionally, is to try to frighten with eerie sounds, disembodied voices, and spooky lighting: devices that cheapen and reduce the significance of the ghost.

Hamlet's father, despite all the "ghostly" terms invoked ("apparition," "illusion," "goblin damn'd," etc.), is real to Hamlet, and was real to Shakespeare and his Elizabethan audience. What is frightening about a ghost is not its unearthliness, but its earthliness: its semblance of reality divorced from existence.

For a man locked in a fantasy, *real* and *unreal* are meaningless terms. Everything that enters his perceptions is real *for him*. In the collage, the dead king is mixed with the living king and then again with the player-king; the dead father with the stepfather; the faithless mother with the seemingly faithless mistress; the past with the present; the actual with the illusory. Such a mixture poses certain questions about the characters of the kings, the live one and the dead one, that are never adequately dealt with in the play.

King Hamlet: this rasping, vengeful old codger who ruled a kingdom already rotten—for the corruption at court certainly existed before Claudius ever came to the throne; this vindictive old shade demanding retribution from beyond the grave—not to test Hamlet's mettle, but because his son is the only means by which he can exact vengeance. He needs a living tool to do his work in the living world, and his son is the obvious choice.

But what kind of king was he? Ruler of a war-torn state; advancer of toads like Polonius; husband to a vain, fickle creature like Gertrude; father of a wishy-washy son who, if he'd had either the gumption or the guile, could have been ruler after his father. How did Claudius manage—so conveniently—to pop in "between th' election and [Hamlet's] hopes?" (One thinks of Trotsky neglecting to return to Moscow after Lenin's death, while Stalin "popp'd in between th' election" and *his* hopes.)

Everything we discern about the dead king and the kingdom he bequeathed throws doubt upon his character. Horatio tells us "this side of our known world esteem'd him valiant," but that is a military attribute, and it is the Norwegian wars Horatio is referring to. As for his moral virtues, apart from his own biased comparison with Claudius, "a wretch whose gifts were poor To those of mine," we have only the word of his bleating son, and we know from his behavior with Ophelia and Gertrude how changeable *his* nature is.

In fact, Hamlet is a poor judge of most people in the play—not because he is thick, but because, being the most subjective character in world drama, he lacks the objectivity to see people clearly. He honestly believes Laertes to be "a very noble youth" and amiably disposed towards him despite the fact that he killed Laertes's father and sent his sister to distraction. Because he thinks Polonius a fool, Polonius *is* a fool when both are together, but when conducting his affairs of state or conversing with his children, there is nothing of the "foolish prating knave" about him.

Hamlet decries the moral side of Claudius's character, but from all we see, Claudius is an efficient monarch and a tactful politician. The crowning irony in Hamlet's bungling misadventures is that, when he finally does dispatch the king, he leaves the country in a worse state than it ever was under Claudius: in the hands of a foreign conqueror whose father was thrashed by Hamlet's father and who has coveted the land ever since. Hamlet hands Fortinbras Denmark on a platter. The patch of ground that he went off to conquer in Poland may have had no profit in it "but the name," but on the way back he gains an entire kingdom without so much as firing a shot. The "damndest defeat" in the play is not Claudius's murder of the king, but the loss of an entire country due to the cantankerous neurosis of one man who wasn't up to his job.

Hamlet as Buffo

Rosencrantz and Guildenstern! Was ever a vaudeville team better named? And was the spirit of vaudeville ever better expressed than in exchanges such as:

HAMLET:
> Good lads; how do ye both?

ROSENCRANTZ:
> As the indifferent children of the earth.

GUIILDENSTERN:
> Happy in that we are not over-happy;
> On Fortune's cap, we are not the very button.

HAMLET:
> Nor the soles of her shoe?

ROSENCRANTZ:
> Neither, my Lord.

HAMLET:
> Then you live about her waist, or in the middle of her favours?

GUILDENSTERN:
> Faith, her privates, we.

HAMLET:
> In the secret parts of Fortune? Oh, most true; she is a strumpet.

The comedy in Hamlet is imbued with music hall. The grave-diggers are almost too blatantly straight-man and comic, and Osric is a satirical extravagance put in at the last moment to lighten the heavy weather of the play's finale. Even Hamlet, in his more manic moments, sinks to punnery and burlesque. In the collage, the comedy has been both concentrated and exaggerated. The two faces of Polonius have been incorporated literally. The same actor, cutting between two distinct characterizations, plays both Polonius and a character called

Clown, which is made up from the gravediggers' quips and cribs from other characters' speeches.

The image of the recorders is basic to Hamlet's relationship with Rosencrantz and Guildenstern, and I have tried to externalize it by showing Hamlet playing and being played upon. A jumping rope links Rosencrantz and Guildenstern, the Bobbsey Twins of Shakespearean tragedy. They are as inseparable as the front and back ends of a vaudeville horse. Hamlet manipulates the rope (or rides the horse) both to amuse himself and to indulge his cruelty. When he is with Rosencrantz and Guildenstern, we catch glimpses of the prankster of Wittenberg: the instigator of university rags and the buoyant under-graduate. When he turns against them, we see the adult meting out the only revenge he successfully dispatches—although even in dis-posing of Rosencrantz and Guildenstern, he relies on forgeries and intermediaries rather than direct personal action. Significantly, he allows them no "shriving time"—precisely the sin he condemns in Claudius's murder of his father.

Open Letter to Horatio

Dear Horatio,

I know the world esteems you a "good friend," but in my opinion you are a rotter. A good friend doesn't let *his* good friend continually delude himself. A good friend says: "You've got everything on your side, and if you kill the king and wrest control, everyone will support you, but if you continue to indulge in amateur theatricals and walk around with your head up your ass you will lose what small dignity you still possess."

You are the most obnoxious yes man in the Shakespearean canon. I suspect that, at base, you are a career opportunist. If your loquacious aristocratic schoolmate ever gains control in Denmark, your future is assured. (No doubt you have your eye on the Ministry of Education.) It isn't until the last moments that you realize you have been backing the wrong horse, and I wonder to what extent your passionate moans for the dying prince are a grandstand play for the new king. I loathe your muttering obsequiousness, your "Aye, my lord" and "No, my lord" and "Is't possible, my lord?"

It is no wonder Hamlet thinks so highly of you. You possess the very same fault that cripples him: the inability to permit conviction to give birth to action. You lack the moral gumption that makes a man forsake fruitless intellectual roundabouting for the sharp, straight path of direct action. To say that your "blood and judgement are so well commingled, That they are not a pipe for Fortune's finger, To sound what stop she please" is only another way of saying there is no impulse so naturally overwhelming that you would not be able to rationalize its reversal or abandonment. Not being "Passion's slave" is one thing, but being so devoid of passion that every rapier thrust is converted to a pin prick is just elaborate hypocrisy. It is a fancy way of saying that the mind is so much the master of the heart that nothing can be truly felt that is not fully understood, and since honor is more a matter of the heart than of the mind, that is just an excuse for evasion and cowardice.

The Lord Hamlet loves you for those very qualities that prove his undoing. Like you, he is one that suffers all yet suffers nothing—since sufferance that doesn't lead to remedy is suffering nothing. Like you, he takes fortune's buffets and rewards with equal thanks. Fortune has deprived him of a kingdom; he makes no move to recover it. Fortune has besmirched the memory of his father; and amidst much breastbeating and verbosity, he accepts the new dispensation. Fortune sends him to England; he goes. Fortune wafts him back; he returns. Fortune has him killed in a duel; and he *defies augury* by walking straight into the trap.

If the old adage is true and one can read people by knowing their friends, then you are an accurate gauge of Hamlet's inadequacies. I have excised you from my *Hamlet*, since you simply hang around like an insufferable feed, wasting pedantry on soldiers who couldn't give a damn, and making false bravura gestures such as drinking from a poisoned goblet that's already been emptied. I have, however, endowed Fortinbras with a great dollop of the Horatio you should have been in a short conversation piece after the trial scene. I hope you will not take this too personally; but the fact is that until further notice, your services will no longer be required.

Hamlet as Myth

The core of *Hamlet* is not to be found in the *Historica Danica* or the *Histoires Tragiques* of François de Belleforest or Kyd's *Spanish Trage-dy*, but in myths so embedded in human consciousness that no one can trace them to any one source. It is because *Hamlet* is essentially *mythic* that one can weave endless variations on its theme. Shakespeare's play is itself a variation of one or several of those legends that swirl around in every country's subculture. I tried to remember when I first became conscious of *Hamlet*. I suppose it was at school, but I can distinctly remember *knowing Hamlet* long before it was ever trotted out as a required text: knowing it not with total knowledge of each strand in its story but in a kind of grey intuitive way; knowing its aura and its ambiance rather than it itself.

Professor Elphin Jones has worked out a fascinating mythic background to the play, based on the notion of the challenger and the champion: a prehistoric concept that tallies with much of its story. Loosely paraphrased, this is his theory:

The origins of human society are based on the tensions between the dominant male (the bull, the stallion) and the challenging younger males. At an early stage of development, human beings did not realize that the male was involved in procreation. It appeared to them that women alone were responsible for the continuation of the species. Since women were dominant in magic (i.e., effective control of the environment), lasting power could rest only with them. They tamed the young of animals that were killed for food, and probably originated herding.

The magical spirit of growth, of birth and death, was incarnate in woman. She was the fount of power, the totem of rule, the "sacred queen." Consequently, the young males built up, via jostling and other feats of skill, a challenge with which to win the female. Each year they fought for her favors, and the winner became her "sacred king." His conquest represented the strength of the tribe. At the end of the year, he was sacrificed, although he might live if he defeated his challengers.

The Hamlet story, Jones believes, may be an attempt to change from a concept of kingship by marriage to the "sacred queen" to a concept of kingship by inheritance from father to son. Viewed from this standpoint, Hamlet is refusing to accept the usurper-king, although he is king by marriage and is putting himself forward as challenger. But by the time the Hamlet story was going through its Shakespearean permutation, the crime of incest was recognized by the community, and if Hamlet successfully challenges the usurper, he has to marry his mother to be the true "sacred king."

The overtones of the Oedipus conflict that actors and directors have "read into" *Hamlet* are an instinctive grasping of the older myth clinging to the later one. The ambivalence in the Hamlet-Gertrude relationship exists in Shakespeare's play. It is not a "psychological imposition." Shakespeare, in his inspired and eclectic way, was using different strands of the same story, unavoidably mixing mythic subtexts by "bringing up to date" older material.

Perhaps it is this mixing up of irreconcilable myths that produced in Hamlet that "emotion" which, according to T. S. Eliot, is "inexpressible because it is in excess of the facts as they appear." "Hamlet," says Eliot, "is up against the difficulty that his disgust is occasioned by his mother, but that his mother is not an adequate equivalent for it; his disgust envelops and exceeds her. It is thus a feeling which he cannot understand; he cannot objectify it, and it therefore remains to poison life and obstruct action. None of the possible actions can satisfy it; and nothing Shakespeare can do with the plot can express Hamlet for him. . . ." But if the *inexpressible* is the dilemma that the challenger cannot oust the usurper without committing incest through marriage with the "sacred queen," then that is a crisis that truly cannot be objectified, as it was as indiscernible to Shakespeare as it was to Hamlet.

Hamlet, in ritualistic terms, has to find a new ground for challenge, and a new myth on which to base his kingship. The new ground for challenge is retribution, justice for the murdered king, punishment for his murderers. The new basis for kingship must be the son's inheritance of the father's crown lost through treachery. That, of course, poses another problem for Hamlet, and one that makes Hamlet's mythic dilemma even more "inexpressible," for if the present king has triumphed through treachery, the queen is implicated and, if retribution follows, is sure to be discredited.

The old-king-new-king-champion-challenger tension in Hamlet may represent, in mythic terms, an attempt to change the tribe's method of creating a new king. The original Hamlet story may well have been based on a myth that either records an attempt to change the rules of kingship, or represents a myth put out as propaganda designed to create respectable reasons for a change in precedent that had already taken place. By the time the story got down to Shakespeare, it was just an anecdote, on a par with fairytales or ancient parables. Shakespeare, in his reworking of the story, builds in a new set of tensions, conflicts derived from his own time and (probably) his own life. But the older tensions, the ones ingrained in the myths on which the stories are based, remain to haunt the subtext and perhaps produce the "intractable material" so many critics complain of.

The answer is not to apply unlimited scholarship to track down the sources of the play, wherever in history or prehistory they may be hiding, but to accept that an old story is rooted in mysteries that never really disappear and which have to be rejigged in order to translate effectively into the present. A cut-up version of *Hamlet*, we may contend, has nothing to do with the play Shakespeare wrote, even if it does utilize his words and many of his ideas. But we can just as readily ask to what extent Shakespeare can be counted the author of a play that is compounded of ancient group myths and cultural *bubumeinshes*, as well as being obviously culled from two or three verifiable, non-Shakespearean sources.

I do not say that to belittle Shakespeare's achievement, but surely the gradations are endless. If a story is root material plus reworking plus an author's viewpoint, then a play is all that plus directorial interpretation and the further transmutations of audience make-up, time of presentation, etc. There is a great deal in *Hamlet* that Shakespeare cannot be held accountable for but that nevertheless exists and must be dealt with in retelling the tale. When a play gets "handed down" from generation to generation over a period of four hundred years, it ends up with a great number of fingerprints on it. Smudge is part of art.

Somewhere in Elsinore

It is a very limited view of reality that contends that a play must take place in a concrete setting; it is almost like saying that life "takes place" in one's home, whereas we know that *where* we are is always a secondary consideration to who we think we are and what we happen to be feeling. We may start a job interview in a plush West End office, but in a moment's time we are operating from some inner, indeterminate point deep in our own being, which may be as threadbare as a derelict shack in a shanty town. And summoned to a hospital waiting room to be given news of life or death, we are equally in a torture chamber, a blind alley, and a bottomless pit. Similarly, in *Hamlet*, the king and queen may well be in the court of Denmark, but their son is located in an elaborate private maze threaded with doubts and resentments. Although Hamlet begins the Closet Scene in his mother's bedchamber, once he is immersed in painful comparisons between the dead king and his stepfather he is in some less distinguishable place, poised between the present and the past; and when the ghost arrives on the scene, he is transferred to yet another plane, perhaps damp with cold and smelling of battlements.

Yes, you may say, but these are different states of mind that occur in every scene and change in almost every speech. Surely it is for the actor to convey all that through his art, and it is idiotic to suggest there be as many locales as there are inner shifts of character. Although that is true, the fact remains that tangible settings perpetuate physical locales when the scene has shifted to other, more significant planes. And when, for instance, the dramatic reality of a scene suggests barrenness and desolation, the sight of settings and furniture cannot be blotted out of a spectator's mind as easily as it can from the character's.

Is it not possible to use the theatre to reflect states of mind more accurately—not simply by removing settings but by implementing the space of the stage so that its visual elements convey psychic moods, not only "period" environment and physical locations? If a room could disappear on the stage at the very moment that it fades out of a character's awareness, an audience would be given a precise, dramatic indication of an internal state. If a house could reflect the transformations that a character experiences in that house, something of the permutations of our inner selves would be shown on the stage.

When we use expressions such as "the ground opened up beneath me," "walking on air," "lost in the clouds," "flipped his lid," "knocked for a loop," "went off his head," we are instinctively employing symbolic language to convey real but indefinable inner states. It is these states that the theatre must learn to convey visually.

This delineation of interior reality is second nature to the *nouveau roman* and is happening everywhere in films. In *The Red Desert*, for instance, Antonioni uses color for its emotive rather than its realistic effect. In Truffaut and Resnais, subliminal flashes are continually used to illustrate inner thoughts and provide subtextual counterpoints to the main action. In certain Happenings in New York and Paris, members of an audience wander through environments that literally transform before their eyes. In the best of these "events," the effect is of *being part of* the permutations happening around us. In the theatre, it would be like having a new vantage point on an emotional change, an internal rather than a topographical view of what is happening inside a character. Obviously, in a realistic play, that could be both chi chi and irrelevant, but as the theatre is hightailing it away from realism, it must inevitably learn this other, newly evolving language.

I loathe theatre scenery, because it is like a phonograph record caught in a groove; it repeats itself endlessly while the play progresses. No scenery I have ever seen can keep up with the progress of a play such as *Hamlet* because it really takes place in the actors' and spectators' shifting consciousness. That is the best place to stage any play. It doesn't rule out the set designer, it simply directs him away from predetermined choices and into an area he knows very little about: an area where color, texture, object, and shape dramatize interior rather than exterior reality; where simultaneity of visual effects produces chords as sonorous and as exciting as those in modern music.

Tips for Set Designers re the Collage

Hamlet takes place *in* Hamlet. We see sights because they are reflected through Hamlet's sensibility. Elsinore is a figment of Hamlet's imagination; so are Gertrude, Claudius, and the ghost. So is poetry; so is comedy; so are pleasure and pain. Hamlet's cerebrum is our cyclorama, his forehead our proscenium arch. The recesses of Hamlet's mind are our flies. An "interior" is not simply the "inside of a room," but the inner perspective of the people who inhabit that room. A color is an emotional hue. An object is as large or small, as real or fantastical, as a character's perception dictates. Ignore all textual stage directions. Have a long drink with the actors playing the main roles. Urge them to discuss their characters; to exaggerate; to use personal imagery; to be far-fetched. Base all your choices on their instincts.

Hamlet and Discontinuity

Since films and novels use it all the time, we should be accustomed to discontinuity, but the theatre, so long in the marble clutches of

Aristotle, finds it impossible to function except chronologically. Sometimes, of course, it resorts to flashbacks or flash-forwards, but these have become adjuncts to the unities, not alternatives.

The most persuasive argument against the formalism of beginning, middle, and end is that it is not truthful. Our lives simply do not unfold like that. Their rhythms are erratic; their points of focus varied and unpredictable; their time structure, if not actually broken, psychologically disjointed and confused. In a time of fission, we cannot accept art that is homogeneous—not if we expect art truthfully to reflect our lives.

Life today (I am not philosophizing, merely trying to illustrate) is very much like the front page of a daily newspaper. The eye jumps from one story to another, from one geographical location to another, from one mood to another: a fire in Hoboken, an election in Paris, a coronation in Sweden, a rape in London, comedy, passion, trivia—all flooding our consciousness almost simultaneously. The writer, however, and the actor after him with centuries of tradition behind him, moves solidly from point A to point B to point C. His characters are *established*, his relationships *develop*, his plot thickens, and his conflicts, resolve. In short, he plods on in his Aristotelian way, perpetuating the stock jargon of drama and the arbitrary time system of the conventional theatre.

The fundamental problem of theatrical discontinuity is communication. If you decide to tell a story about a man throwing over his wife and marrying his daughter, and decide to convey it through random and arbitrary flashes from that man's life, it is quite possible no one will understand your story. You have removed the narrative frame of reference, prevented an audience from meeting your characters and watching them develop through actions. There is no reason why they should understand sporadic flashes out of a story to which they come as strangers and of which they see nothing but disconnected bits.

And yet, disconnected bits are all we know of most people's stories, with the possible exception of our own. We piece together information, hunches, guesses, lies, and hearsay about everyone we know. Our much-touted "understanding" of people is simply this eclectic, incomplete, second-hand hodgepodge of poorly filtered data. In life, narrative is the accumulation of discontinuous events spread over a long period of time, eventually assembled into a story.

Dramatic art has, for centuries, been doing the same thing, except that in wedging its material into a preexisting form (Aristotelian play structure), it has unavoidably falsified its findings. You cannot demonstrate a circle if all you have at your disposal are square blocks. You *can* construct an octagonal shape and say, "Well, a circle is something like that, only try to imagine all those straight edges rounded off." That is the dilemma of the theatre today: trying with simple and inappropriate forms to convey the elaborate content of our lives. When the content refuses to be restricted within those forms and bursts them apart (as in Happenings, for instance), the pundits cry: "Whatever it is, it's not theatre." Of course it's not. Theatre, as we all know, is something we can assemble within our square blocks. Whatever is difficult to assemble may be "experimental" or "avant-garde," but anything that absolutely resists assembly simply isn't theatre.

Shakespeare's *Hamlet* is a play intended for square blocks. I am not disparaging it. It has been a very good play, and has operated successfully within those blocks and, no doubt, will do so again. But because it has been around so long and is so well known, it is well suited for breaking out of those blocks.

I said before that disconnected bits are all we know of most people's stories except our own. I should add that we know the stories of those people whose bits have been assembled many years ago and frequently recounted. It is because we know the continuity of a play such as *Hamlet* that we are able to experience it discontinuously. More important, by experiencing it discontinuously, we get to know it more intimately, because its rhythms are closer to the ones that whip us through the underground rush hour than the ones that nudged Shakespeare through the hills of Warwickshire.

It is a trap to reiterate mindlessly that human nature remains fairly constant and that because the Elizabethan Age was one of expansion and exploration, and our own time is, too, there is an inescapable similarity between the 1660s and the 1960s. There is—quite literally—a *world* of difference between the 1980s and the 1940s, between the 1950s and the 1930s, and considering the frequency with which nations topple and thought transforms, next month may be the beginning of a completely new millennium, and this month we would not even have a hint of it. The two overriding contemporary facts are speed and change. We have always had change, but now that we have rapid, almost incessant change, we must come to terms with the daily factor of speed: the relentless, insatiable motor power that makes the world move as quickly as it does.

That, circuitously, brings me back to *Hamlet*. A collage technique is a way of transmitting speed in the theatre. It is a speed by which thoughts, actions, locales, and styles can be quickly shuffled. It has nothing to do with *pace*, the mechanical acceleration of Aristotle's "slow time." Its speed is the result of being in many different places in quick succession and without predictable order. Some of these "places" in *Hamlet* are:

The court at Elsinore
A plateau in the superego
The past as distorted by the present
The present as distorted by the past
A circus
An intellectual plane where various pieces of
    Shakespearean criticism commingle
Limbo
Heaven
Hell
A theatre.

Notes on *THE SHREW*

Taming of the Shrew equals *Duchess of Malfi*.

All comedy must be siphoned from the play. The grim implications of Petruchio's behavior against Kate must be, as it were, alienated from the body of the farce and revealed as the true and terrible subject beneath the play's conventional frivolities.

When Petruchio comes to his "wedding," he wears an exact duplicate of the wedding gown being worn by Kate. His "costume" makes a travesty not only of the marriage ceremony but of the traditional dignity associated with the bride.

When Petruchio takes Katherine away to his manor, the spirit of John Webster routs that of William Shakespeare. In his manor, a kind of medieval dungeon created and manned by servants who have been especially rehearsed to disorient Kate, the brainwashing begins. When the manor doors are shut, Kate's fate is sealed.

Petruchio would inflict these subtle tortures on Kate even if he didn't stand to gain a penny. The torturer or sadistic prison guard is there not for money but to indulge the innate cruelty of his nature. The torture chamber, with its parade of pathetic victims, is part of his peculiar gestalt. It enables him to "get his rocks off" while at the same time pretending to perform a socially useful function.

What Kate learns from Petruchio is that dominance has nothing to do with intellectual superiority. A quick wit, a fertile intellect, a higher sense of breeding mean nothing when you are sleepy, starving, and physically menaced. The virtues of civilized society evaporate when you descend into a primitive world where animal appetite and physical domination prevail. There are no satirists in a concentration camp.

Interspersed between crucial scenes of Shakespeare's play (mainly those concerning Petruchio and Kate) is a series of contemporary scenes. The characters in these scenes are a young man and a young woman, loosely extrapolated from Lucentio and Bianca. The girl is upper-middle-class, sophisticated, feminist in the sense that she experiences her own independence; *un*feminist in that she feels no compulsion to demonstrate it. The boy is what we would call upwardly mobile; a working-class youth with middle-class ambitions. He is fascinated by the girl, mainly because she personifies a social stratum and a lifestyle to which he (unavowedly) aspires.

They meet. They take to each other. They coalesce. Their relationship begins to experience stresses. It gradually deteriorates. It becomes asphyxiating. They marry. All of these scenes are interlarded between those Shakespearean scenes that depict the developing relationship of Petruchio and Kate. As Petruchio overmasters Kate and suborns her will, the girl (Bianca) dominates and overwhelms the young man (Lucentio) until she is herself dominated by what both of them have become: mutual prisoners of "the relationship." Kate is utterly and abysmally defeated and achieves a kind of martyrdom therefrom. The young man and woman mutually create a kind of Frankenstein monster, which lives with them for the rest of their days. Their dungeon is called marriage, and because their incarceration is virtually indistinguishable from so many others, they assume anguish and emptiness are the norm. They live "happily ever after"—that is, they couple and quarrel, fabricate and dissipate, each day fraying a little more the already fragile thread of their ill-fated love affair.

The thematic problems of *The Shrew* became clearer and clearer each time we played it. The parallel scenes were too baldly parallel to the Petruchio and Kate scenes, and the message that seemed to screech out of the modern scenes in which Bianca domineered and manipulated Lucentio was that nothing very much had changed since the seventeenth century; that cruelty and power play were still the active components of relationships. Whereas in the good old days, the man could brutalize the woman using physical means, today the woman could tyrannize the man using the more subtle weapons of psychology and social exploitation. Clearly, that was a statement not worth making—and certainly not worth cutting up a Shakespearean play in order to make.

What was needed was a careful reassessment of the play's ideology, or, rather, the ideology of the contemporary scenes—for that was where the trouble lay. I did not intend to say that things never change, that cruelty between human beings is a constant factor that alters only its methods but not its intentions. What I wanted to say was, in fact, much more dismal and depressing, namely: that no human relationship has the stamina to withstand long periods of intimate exposure; that familiarity breeds not only contempt but dissipation and stasis; that deep within the very fabric of human relationships—relationships founded on love and togetherness—there was an insidious canker that slowly but surely gnawed away at the euphoria that infused every love affair; that there was something at the core of human nature that was irrevocably abusing and self-consuming, and that the irony of this cancer was that it lurked quietly but potently in a context of love, watching love recede and gradually growing bolder and bolder until ultimately it conquered all.

And, irony of ironies, it was at this very juncture that the diseased lovers often sought in the institution of marriage a kind of miracle drug that would miraculously restore the pristine state. One wanted to show that for many people, despite the raging permissiveness of our times, marriage, the hoked-up, endlessly spoofed magic ritual, still held out a promise of salvation—a hope that the formal pantomime of an ancient ceremony could transform a grubby reality; that a solemn rite could, by virtue of its intrinsic magic, right the wrongs of years.

To tell such a story, Shakespeare's combative couple had to leave the realms of farce and transmute themselves into a kind of Grimm fairytale world, a world of sinister archetypes and hopeless victims. Petruchio, transformed into a kind of Mafioso monster who still covets Baptista's fortune and is fully prepared to instigate a bloodless courtship to obtain it, is now motivated even more strongly by the detestable independence of spirit that throbs inside of Katherine. The confrontation between this Petruchio and this Kate is a classic encounter of elegance and vulgarity rather than female high-spiritedness and the urge for male conquest.

The tragedy of Kate, in this new dispensation, is that she underestimates the magnitude of Petruchio's bestiality. How could she not? The rich daughter of a rich father; the recipient of, if not love, then certainly luxury, education, and breeding? Compare such a woman to a strolling fortune hunter who goes sniffing for rich game and makes no distinction between material gain and amoristic conquest; for whom, indeed, the latter is only a means of acquiring the former. A wastrel, a bogus cavalier; a man who never read Castiglione but who knows that the only way to get on in the world is to emulate his type. A man whose peculiar psychosis insists on total subservience as the emblem of love; who counterfeits with the grim, convincing deportment of the crypto-psychopath; who embodies and glories in those characteristics that Wilhelm Reich attributes to the phallic narcissist.

The modern technique for brainwashing is, almost to the letter, what Petruchio makes Katherine undergo. Deprivation of food, deprivation of sleep, disorientation of faculties; cruelty camouflaged as kindness; a reversal of moral values that turns the tormenter into a holy man and the tormented into a hopeless sinner. Petruchio's evil genie punishes Katherine for the greatest crime of all—sexual rebellion. A woman she can be, she must be, but not *her* kind of woman— rather, the social cipher that Baptista prefers, that Bianca unquestionably is, that Lucentio would have all women be, that Petruchio labors to create.

If Katherine can be made to represent breeding and elegance, and we are able to discard the tirades of the traditional termagant, her downfall becomes truly pathetic, for it then represents the abandonment of personal style in the face of a brutalizing conformity. If she is shrilly vituperative and conventionally shrewish (Elizabeth Taylor swinging frying pans), then all she gets is comeuppance, and the conventional charade of subterranean longings for Petruchio clears the way for her wholesale conversion to domesticity—a conversion that, in my view, is never alleviated by a tang of irony in the final speech before the wives. Katherine accepts nothing and struggles against her cruel punishment to the very end. The only victory available to the Petruchio-Baptista-Bianca axis is the artificially induced spectacle of a mesmerized or drugged victim droning the words her tormenters could not make her speak voluntarily. A victory of these dimensions is hollow indeed.

What rots Katherine is the quicklime of Petruchio's spirit. What rots the young man and woman in the contemporary scenes is the indeterminate moral pollution that many would blame on the social context but whose toxins are discharged through the pores of the human beings who constitute that society. There is no villain or villainess in the contemporary scenes. Whatever personal failings Lucentio and Bianca may have, they are typical, not unique. What happens to them happens to many people. Their "tragedy," if you like, is built into their human metabolism. They can never escape, and their danger is never, like Katherine's, apparent and challengeable.

Katherine is felled by the will of a destructive force she can feel and see. She knows where to do battle, and she does so valiantly—right up to the very end. Lucentio and Bianca in the contemporary scenes go through the motions of living and loving, of jealousy and possessiveness, of separations and reunions—like experimental mice that caper and cavort, feed and defecate, but whose destiny is sealed the moment they enter their laboratory cages. I am not alluding here to anything as simple as predestination. Perhaps there *is* another way out for Bianca and her young man; perhaps marriage will replenish their love-cells, but as we see them, they haven't the power to do anything more than feed off each other, try to elude boredom, hope for transformations in their inner lives, and, ultimately, settle for less—the inescapable twentieth-century compromise.

Bianca and her mate in their scenes have quarrels, but Katherine fights for her life. The young couple dwindle into social statistics; Katherine's defeat defines the grandeur of a spirit that has been brought down by overwhelming odds. There is something noble in that defeat, because in its resistance, an alternative way of life, a higher degree of individuality, has been implied. Bianca and beau gradually disappear into the feckless, wholly expedient, mutually exploitative morass of modern life. It is hard to say, viewed that way, which represents the greater tragedy.

Despite its nastiness, despite its taken-for-granted subjugation of women, despite its overriding male chauvinist outlook, there is in the deepest subsoil of Shakespeare's *Taming of the Shrew* the seeds of the most feminist play written in the seventeenth century. It may have taken four centuries for it to sprout, but nothing sprouts that is not first planted.

Notes on a Midsummer Night's Dream

A Midsummer Night's Dream: Story of the Play

Oberon, a vindictive homosexual chieftain who exerts immense authority among his circle of followers in the forest, has tried repeatedly to wrest a beautiful Indian boy from his former lover, now rival, Titania. Titania's refusal to give up the youth or share him with others (the established sexual convention) has incensed Oberon and caused irremediable friction between the two camps.

To wreak the revenge burning in his bosom, Oberon arranges through Puck, an old and embittered slave, to administer a potent aphrodisiac to Titania, which causes him to become sexually obsessed with the first creature he encounters. Because of Puck's age and incompetence (and the imprecise nature of Oberon's instructions), the drug also is given to two of the four refugees who have wandered into the wood to escape arbitrary measures meted out by the state. That causes a series of promiscuous embroglios, wholly uncharacteristic of the four persons involved.

Eventually, through guile, Oberon manages to appropriate the boy for himself, and Titania, now caught in the spell of the aphrodisiac, becomes enamored with an actor, one of several rehearsing a play in the forest, who has been transformed into a beast by the vicious

Puck. Having now acquired the coveted youth, Oberon takes pity on Titania's condition and releases him from the spell, and the old sharing homosexual relationship is restored.

The wood, now transformed into an erotic labyrinth, impels the lovers to pursue their carnal and licentious desires until Puck lifts their spell. Once returned to Athens, freed from the diabolical influence of the wood and no longer forced into arbitrary bonding, the lovers settle back to enjoy the entertainment laid on for the duke's wedding, but Puck, in a final act of vindictiveness, upsets the performance of the play, terrorizes the wedding guests, and reminds them that despite their contentment and return to normalcy, nefarious, antisocial spirits such as he are the true rulers of the world.

At its deepest level, *The Dream* is a play about forbidden fruits: promiscuity, bestiality, the slaking of carnal appetites, all those irresistible and primitive desires society firmly represses in order to insure an orderly perpetuation. Midsummer Night, as the Scandinavians know better than most, is a night of unmitigated revelry, in which the most potent sexual and antisocial cravings are released. Shakespeare, being a bourgeois writing for a partly bourgeois public, had to cloak the expression of these pernicious desires within the framework of "a dream" to make them acceptable, but it is a thin disguise, and the whiff of amorality fairly wafts through the musk and foliage.

Love in idleness is an aphrodisiac. "Idleness" means going nowhere, unproductive, unfruitful—sex for fun and not for procreation. Puck, a character derived from an ancient medieval devil, is the incarnation of our most demonic nature; an otherworldly spirit exempt from social restraints who encourages our id to run riot over our ego.

He is in the employ of an even more nefarious spirit, Oberon—the Ruler of the Night, the King of the Fairies; a kind of psychopathic sexual tyrant whose life is devoted to base practices and the satisfaction of unnatural appetites. His conflict with Titania, a former lover, is due to the fact that he-she has flouted the rules of their ravenous society by refusing to share pleasures normally considered communal—i.e., the desired Indian boy. It is the collision between these primal natures and the civilized youths of Athens (whose own desires are frustrated by parents and the state) that occurs in the wood. They are drawn into a world of license and sensuality that is the moral opposite of their conventional society founded on repression and monogamy.

The mechanicals, simple tradespeople preparing a performance tribute for the duke's nuptials, are much closer to free nature than the pretentious, upper-middle-class personages who, during the marriage entertainment, mock and ridicule them, but for whom they still maintain a misguided respect. Bottom's transformation into an ass is only one step down from the simple-minded rustic one-with-nature creature he already is. He and his fellows are the representatives of those economically dependent lower orders from which aristocrats traditionally drew their sexual hirelings, and in turning to him for satisfaction, Titania's behavior is entirely in keeping with the class practices of Elizabethan society.

The simplicity, lack of sophistication, and oneness with nature personified by the mechanicals stand in direct contrast to the devious, manipulative, sexually motivated characters of Oberon, Titania, and the lovers. Theseus, the reigning spirit of the play's connubial life, has won Hippolyta's love through colonization. ("I wooed thee with my sword/And won thy love with injuries.") She is the spoils of his victory—a conquest—no tenderness—no reciprocal courtship— merely a trophy for a victor. Perhaps the reason Hippolyta says so little is that she resents the usurpation of her womanly and deific rights. In Theseus's appropriation of Hippolyta, there is the echo of Oberon's original appropriation of Titania and his possessive attitude to the Indian boy. Before the present distribution of sexual partners, we know that Oberon is supposed to have lusted after Hippolyta even as Titania did after Theseus.

TITANIA:
    Why art thou here
    Come from the farthest steep of India?
    But that forsooth, the bouncing Amazon,
    Your buskined mistress and your warrior-love
    To Theseus must be wedded, and you come
    To give their bed joy and prosperity.

OBERON:
    How canst thou thus for shame, Titania
    Glance at my credit with Hippolyta,
    Knowing I know thy love to Theseus?

Didst thou not lead him through the glimmering night
From Perigenia, whom he ravished?
And make him with fair Aegles break his faith,
With Ariadne and Antiopa?

The whole background of the play is one of rampant promiscuity and swapping of sexual partners, which we associate with the most decadent societies.

Puck is an old, cantankerous, and cruel flunky whose only delight is creating confusion and moral disarray. Like Ariel, whom he resembles, he is Oberon's recidivist—a "lifer" who, unlike Prospero's sprite, can never have his sentence commuted. He is doomed to sow seeds of dissension among the bitchy, vindictive creatures that inhabit Oberon's and Titania's underworld. He is very *un*-airborne. He talks about "putting a girdle round about the earth in forty minutes," but that is empty braggadocio, a pathetic throwback to the alacrity and fleet-footedness he once had but has long lost. He lumbers, he plods, he bitches, and he moans. He's a thoroughly fed-up and frustrated hireling who gets a small amount of delight from riot and catastrophe but is constitutionally world-weary and has seen it all.

The lovers are members of that smug, privileged upper-middle-class set that approvingly accepts Theseus and Hippolyta as the king-pin and queenpin (respectively) of their court. (This society is clearly founded on the euphoria of recent military victories.) When they are themselves, they play at romance and courtship, blithely circulating from one lover's bed to the other. (Demetrius allegedly "made love" to Helena before becoming besotted with Hermia, and Lysander effortlessly switches to Helena under the influence of a mesmerizing aphrodiasiac, but, as we know, persons under hypnosis can perform only acts basically consistent with their character.) The lure of the wood and the spell of the drug merely release the lust and lechery that were always there. When they sober up in the forest after Puck has lifted the spell, they cling desperately to the theory that they have been asleep ("Let's follow him, and by the way recount our dreams"), for only in the throes of fantasy can they justify the ravenous nature of their illicit drives.

The tumult in the world ("These are the forgeries of jealousy," etc.) that results from Oberon's feud with Titania is the conflict of the ordered universe confounded by the spirit of anarchy, and its concomitant is untrammeled sexuality. There is an even deeper reverberation: the opposition between heterosexual love and homosexual license. Oberon, Titania, and their followers represent the homosexual oligarchy, which flourished and held sway before heterosexuality became the dominant sexual fashion. The phantoms of that older order still cling to the underside of life, and, though active only under cover of darkness, they manage to exert their influence and project treacheries against the new social order.

Behind the traditional facade of lyricism and romantic love usually thrown up around this play, there is the undertow of an eroticism that bound man to man more fervently than it ever drew together the opposite sexes. That, in my view, is the part of *The Dream* that has eluded detection for over four hundred years; the bestiality, the rustic romps through deregulated terrains, the vague sense of orgy and riot that issues from the now-forbidden love of man for man constantly subvert the rosy-colored image of heterosexual harmony that was the cover story not only of Elizabethan theatre but of Elizabethan life as well.

11

Dialogue with
Glenda Jackson

In the mid-sixties, when I was instructed by Peter Brook to come up with a group of twelve actors that might compose the Royal Shakespeare Company Experimental Group, I first came across Glenda Jackson. Her audition for the so-called Theatre of Cruelty Season (an ensemble effort devoted to exploring the ideas of Antonin Artaud, which spawned a production of Genet's *The Screens* and ultimately Peter Weiss's *Marat/Sade*) was memorable, to say the least. One sensed behind her work a frenetic power that put her in a different class from the discreet, well-spoken actresses that flocked to those unpredictable and unorthodox workouts. When the twelve came to be chosen, it was a toss-up whether Glenda would be cast. There was strong advocacy within the R.S.C. for another actress who also had a remarkable talent. But I had been so captivated by the inventive surge of her improvisations, the daring of her choices, and the nutty energy that smoldered under her neurotic exterior that I went forcibly to bat for her, and fortunately Brook, who shared my enthusiasm, concurred.

I mention this incident only to show that my relationship with Glenda goes back to those days when she was simply a talented stage actress with no hint of the superstar status to come. Since then, in my capacity as roving drama critic, I have often been impelled to rap her knuckles or whack her backside and have wriggled at her excesses almost as often as I have flipped at her triumphs. Talent notwithstanding, she is one of the few actresses I know who can speak articulately about the art of acting, and since no book about directing can be complete without including the actor's view of the director's role, I chose to include a dialogue that does just that. It ranges a bit into other areas, as all shoptalk must, but essentially it provides a coherent view of the interpretative process from the standpoint of an actress who does it remarkably well.

The following is an edited verbatim transcript of a talk we had in New York City in the spring of 1985, where she was appearing in Eugene O'Neill's *Strange Interlude.*

MAROWITZ:

What do you look to get from a director?

JACKSON:

This is a very difficult question for me to answer, really, because I think there are a great many people who call themselves directors, and indeed are employed as directors, and really can't direct. If we are talking about what one looks for from a *good* director, of which there are only about three in the world, it is someone who waits to see what you are going to do, who can create a climate which is not boring and in which you are actually productive, and who knows very early on what he doesn't want—which is rather more valuable than knowing what he does want.

MAROWITZ:

Is the director's conception something that you feel you ought to be privy to right from the start, and is it a factor in whether or not you undertake a role?

JACKSON:

Oh, yes, I think so. For example, I recently did *Phaedre,* which Philip Prowse directed. Now, Philip had a very clear view of how the play should look, and on the first day we were presented with the set, which clearly gave us his concept of the play. And I, as we all did, acknowledged that we had to make our work function in that setting. When we actually came to rehearse the acting part of it, he was very clear in his own mind about the kind of images he wanted to see on the stage. Where he wasn't so good from an actor's point of view was that he didn't understand that actors have to find the bridges *between* the images. They have to make it all up. It all has to have an inner logic for the actor.

MAROWITZ:

To what extent does the inner logic of a role depend on the performer, and to what extent does it depend on collaboration between a director and a performer? Does a director have any kind of jurisdiction over the mapping out of that inner logic?

JACKSON:

I would have thought probably not, really. However, your inner logic can be absolutely clear for you and, at the same time, a terrible brake on the play's function. Sometimes it can stop the play flowing. Especially if you are too pedantic about what the character would or would not do. So good directors say: "Fine, hang onto the inner logic, but you have to find another way around because *this* is what the play actually needs here."

MAROWITZ:

In other words, the logic of the performer really has to connect to the overriding logic of the production.

JACKSON:

Absolutely. And your character has to function with other characters, and they all have to function with a "play." Then the "play" presumably has to function within a sense of what the director wants that play to do or say.

MAROWITZ:

Have you ever found yourself in a situation where you were completely at odds with the interpretation being foisted by a director?

JACKSON:

Yes, but not since I have been in the position to choose what I want to do. There are two very clear examples I've had in my experience, both when I was with the R.S.C. One was doing *Love's Labour's Lost* with John Barton, and the other was doing *Puntila and His Servant Matti* with Michel St. Denis. Both directors, in their different ways, had already run for themselves an absolutely perfect production. St. Denis used to come to work armed with a hundred battle plans. Each character had a color. He would stop a rehearsal and say, "Where are you now?" And you would say, "I'm here." And he would say, "No, no, you should be two inches further to the left." And that was, for me, a crucifying experience. I found that an impossible way of working. In *Love's Labour's Lost,* John Barton was essentially concerned with the sound of the play, onto which he stuck what seemed to me utterly inorganic moves, groupings, and bits of business, none of which (my memory is a little foggy now) had actually been discovered by the actors.

MAROWITZ:

Now, in both of those cases, the "fault," if you like, would seem to be that the director had fully premeditated his result before the rehearsal process began.

JACKSON:

Yes.

MAROWITZ:

Is this a kind of curse in the theater, the director who comes to the first rehearsal with a clear-cut plan already in mind and is so prepared that, in a sense, there is no room for an actress's original interpretation to intrude?

JACKSON:

I have always felt that I have known a play when I have gone into rehearsal. All I do before the start of rehearsals is read the play a lot, and so I tend to arrive at the room thinking I know it, and invariably my experience has been that I *haven't* known it. I came to discover a whole slate of things about it and about the characters. That is sort of basic, I think, for most productions. The difference, it seems to me, has to do with energy. If a director comes as Barton and St. Denis did, with everything taped, very clear on specifics and how each scene should be expressed, what is never there, in that kind of work situation, is the real energy of the scene. Which is very different from somebody like Peter Brook, who may have no idea at all about the specifics but is absolutely clear on the *kind* of energy that each scene has to pour into an auditorium. He may simply say: "Well, it's just on too small a level. It's very nice but that's not really what the scene is about. The scene is about a clash of titanic forces." Well, if somebody says to you "clash of titanic forces," you already have to look and think in a different way, and what you then find to express *that* is always exciting and interesting and invariably organic.

Whereas if somebody says, oh, you know, "He gives her the letter," or "She kisses his hand," or something, and simply gives you a number of specific actions to perform, I find that utterly demoralizing.

MAROWITZ:

So the director has to be an instigator of energies, and those energies are the ones that are, in a sense, trapped under the scene, and it is the collaboration between the actor and the director that releases them.

JACKSON:

That unlocks it, yes.

MAROWITZ:

But that seems to suggest that the director is not entitled to have already worked out in his mind what he feels the scene is truly about.

JACKSON:

Yes, but then good directors do; but good directors will change their mind, too. I mean, they will come in and say: "You know, I thought it was this, but now, you see, it's that." Whereas bad directors will never give up their battle plans. They will always attempt to make what they saw running in their imaginations, in the privacy of their study while they were reading the play, happen on the stage.

MAROWITZ:

Then the secret, if there is such a thing as a secret, of organic theatrical production is that one should ride the existential moment; that is, try to find out—existentially—what ought to be happening in a scene.

JACKSON:

Yes.

MAROWITZ:

But is it possible for either a director or an actress not to come to a play without fairly clear-cut preconceptions?

JACKSON:

Take a great play; an English classic, let's say. Everybody thinks they know the play by virtue of its longevity. It has been around a very long time. And what I have always found interesting is that when you actually come down to work on it, you *don't* know it. What you know is a lot of received information that has come down over the years. When you actually get down to work on the text, it is often—nine times out of ten—a completely different play in what it is essentially about.

MAROWITZ:

If you're lucky.

JACKSON:

What do you mean, if you're lucky?

MAROWITZ:

If you come to a play that everybody already knows and you discover a new one, you are lucky. If you come to a play that everybody knows and you discover the traditional known quantity, then you are rather unlucky.

JACKSON:

Well, I obviously haven't done enough classical work to be able to counter that argument. In the handful of classic plays that I have done, it's always been my experience that we thought we knew the play and we haven't. We've known what people have told us about the play, but when you come to work on it, something else occurs. I mean, the only real preconception you can have if you're doing a great classic play, or even a good modern play, is that the group of you aren't up to the talent that made the play. Therefore, you should be locked into a realization that the work is going to be hard, elusive, and seriously intended— which means that you are going to have to leave an awful lot of things outside the rehearsal-room door. And if the director believes that, too, then it's terrific. What I felt about both my mishaps—and they're not the only lousy productions I've been in; please don't think that—and I'm not castigating Barton and St. denis for being the only lousy directors; they were just lousy for me, that's all. But the thing is, I don't believe directors like that genuinely respect the play—as such—because they're not willing for it to really take life. I mean to establish its *own* life. There's a kind of feeling in the air that: "This is a great play, therefore it has to be done a certain way." Great plays are great plays because they survive the tampering of idiots over the centuries.

MAROWITZ:

It *is* a cryptic form of arrogance for a director to approach a play with an unwavering preconception—as if to say: "I have come to this work in order to unveil my version of it!"

JACKSON:

To go back to Brook again and our work on *Antony and Cleopatra*: When he came to that play, he was absolutely adamant that the work had to come out of the text. Everything we needed in order to do the play well was *in that text*, and our job was to dig it out, and that was precisely the process, digging out the energy of the play. And it's astonishing, because when you do that successfully, there are nights that you can literally feel the play playing you. It's all there if you will only trust it.

MAROWITZ:

What happens, though, in cases where somebody approaches a classic not simply to enliven *that* text but to bring to it a new conception; a conception which may have more to do with what's going on in contemporary society, let's say, than what is actually going on within the framework of that text?

JACKSON:

I don't think that's possible. Great classic plays are great plays because they tend to be contemporary. By that I mean, there is something in them that always speaks directly to the human condition, which does not seem to me to change very much over the years. The externals change, and they're the first things that an audience sees. By externals I mean sets and costumes. But then, if the work is really good, those are the first things that are forgotten. Those images flash on the retina and they're gone. Then you are actually into the business of: what are these people *really* about, what is this play *really* about?!

MAROWITZ:

What you seem to be saying is the only way to have a proper and effective interpretation of a play is to be essentially traditional; that is, to express the meaning of that original play—which would seem to exclude the possibility of bringing new meaning to a play.

JACKSON:

That's not true, actually. I'm obviously not being lucid about it, and I can well understand why, since acting is easier to do than to talk about. But take *Phaedre*, for instance. Now, that was a brand new translation which observed all the constituents of the original French text, setting aside the poetic use of the language, which is virtually impossible to translate. Racine uses, I think, only six hundred words—as did the translator, David MacDonald. The language is really very simple and direct in French, albeit there is some limitation due to the fact that the church didn't allow certain words to be used. Still, given that stricture, Racine manages to put into that two-hour piece a day in the life of the House of Theseus in which the most incredible things happen. It is a great tragedy told very quickly, sparsely, and directly. Which is also what MacDonald did. You can't make it contemporary in today's fashion, which is realistic, naturalistic behavior, because that doesn't work. You have to observe the rules, and the rules are that everything has to work within this text—which is not couched in a realistic, naturalistic way. However, what these people are talking about, what the play is essentially about, remains psychologically true. These are people in the grip of great passions. They don't feel things in a small, mundane way. So given that, and acknowledging that the only means you have to express to an audience what you are feeling is the text, you cannot break up that rhythm. You cannot alter it; you cannot make it colloquial. You have to observe its rules. In a way, that's very liberating, because it means you can concentrate on the one area that matters—which is how to find the right emotional coloration to make clear to an audience that you are not simply mouthing strange Alexandrine verse. That is where *we* were contemporary in our production in England: in finding that contemporary corollary. If the French reports that I read are to be believed, for generations they had opted for doing it the way it was first done. The "contemporary tradition" then was that you stood on a stage and you spoke it beautifully, but that is no longer the contemporary tradition. In believing that was the only way to do it, they ossified the play. But it's a good enough, a true enough, play to work in a contemporary situation.

MAROWITZ:

Since I haven't seen *Phaedre*, it is hard to grasp exactly what you are saying, but it seems the thing that made your production contemporary was that it was infused with "contemporary" feeling, and that contemporary feeling in no way obstructed or violated or did injury to the original text.

JACKSON:

Exactly.

MAROWITZ:

So in order to do a foreign classic in a modern way, we are really talking again about the infusion of a certain kind of energy, and not the alteration of language.

JACKSON:

Absolutely. The energies are there, within the play, if you will just let them out. But if you attempt to impose things from the outside, then you will never release it. And, as I say, you have to observe the rules of the play.

MAROWITZ:

How much do you take from other actors in forming your own performance?

JACKSON:

It's hard to know where the constituent parts come from, but I would think a great deal, really.

MAROWITZ:

Have you ever found yourself in a situation where the inadequacy of certain actors diminished the extent to which you could develop your own performance?

JACKSON:

Yes . . . yes.

MAROWITZ:

If that is the case, does it mean that if you find yourself with very good people who are highly resourceful, that inclines your performance in yet another direction?

JACKSON:

Not necessarily in another direction, but certainly the work, probably, is richer.

MAROWITZ:

Do the precepts of Stanislavsky, the Method, in any way help you in your work?

JACKSON:

> I don't subscribe to the idea that there is *a* method for acting. I do subscribe to the idea, because I believe it to be true, that every actor has their own method, and if it works for the actor, then fine.

MAROWITZ:

> Can you define your own approach to acting? Do you find yourself doing the same kinds of things each time you start work on a role?

JACKSON:

> All I do is read the play a lot. That is all I ever do, and I expect the work to happen at rehearsal. My way, usually, is I'll go for something extreme and then see what happens.

MAROWITZ:

> What about *Strange Interlude*, which I've just recently seen? In the first scenes of that play, we encounter a character who seems to be under great stress and having a bit of a nervous breakdown. Did you choose to play that sense of stress in an "extreme" way?

JACKSON:

> In that particular instance, she is only about nineteen, so I tended to look for the relevant physical expression. If you are in a state of panic or fear or whatever, what is physically happening to you? A great deal of adrenalin suddenly pumps through you. Your heart is pounding. Your palms are sweating. Your breath is shallow. Those kinds of things are the way in for me. I try to find a physical expression of these things on an extreme level and then pull it back.

MAROWITZ:

> Why do you feel it necessary to begin at an extreme level?

JACKSON:

> This is just for me. I am lazy and sometimes a bit secretive. There are certain scenes that I know I will never attempt until I am in the safety of an auditorium with an audience. I will never make myself feel such a fool in a rehearsal room. So the combination of being lazy and a bit secretive means that I have to make extreme choices, because that opens up something for me.

MAROWITZ:

And what you just said opens up something for me, which is: To what extent can a performer fulfill emotional states in a rehearsal situation, and to what extent must the rehearsal situation simply be a preparation for a fulfillment that can only come about when an audience is there?

JACKSON:

Well, I don't think you're asking the right question, in a sense. The experience of the emotion, having decided what it is, or discovered it by virtue of working with other actors on a scene and learning what the scene requires, the general sense of the emotion—all that can only happen in rehearsal. That is where it has to happen. It is only when you get the sense of that and the smell of that—the emotion genuinely felt—that you can begin to act it. When you come to perform, that is, when all those things move to another plane by virtue of performing, which is another process to rehearsal, lots of other things come into play. It has a lot to do with fear and excitement and the added dimension of an audience, which will suddenly make you see something quite a different way or make you realize that what you thought you were giving, you are not. But the actual rehearsal period is the only time you can genuinely feel the emotion. When you come to play it, you are doing something else.

MAROWITZ:

Is the emotion that you play in a performance merely an extension of the emotion you have engendered during rehearsal?

JACKSON:

It's not merely an extension, nor should it really be the same emotion. Experiencing the emotion should, and in my experience does, give you an insight into how to play the scene. It is not enough to "feel" it, because that doesn't go anywhere. That is not what acting is, anyway. That's "being." And if you feel it really, genuinely, you probably can't finish the rest of the play. The value of feeling it in rehearsal is that it opens up something. You think, well, that is what I felt; now out of that feeling what can I take to show *them* what the feeling is like, so that *they* can feel it?

MAROWITZ:

So there is a kind of two-step between the actress feeling emotion and then, in a sense, demonstrating it through theatrical means to an audience?

JACKSON:

Absolutely.

MAROWITZ:

Now, a Method actor or director would say this is heresy; that in fact, it is you experiencing the emotion before an audience that makes it valid to an audience.

JACKSON:

Well, I don't believe that. That seems to me to be a peculiarly convoluted form of hypocrisy. It ignores the fact that you are actually doing a play. I absolutely acknowledge, to go back to the idea of an inner logic, that the world that you create upon that stage has to be absolutely real, but it does not necessarily have to be realistic to *be* real, if you see what I mean.

MAROWITZ:

You mean it can be artificial and real at the same time?

JACKSON:

It has its own reality. That is surely what theatre is. It is a heightened reality. It is life as it should be but hardly ever is. You are making it realistic in its own terms.

MAROWITZ:

Is the truth of what a performer is feeling not the end of the line?

JACKSON:

No, it is the beginning of the line! As I said just now, when you feel it, when you have that genuine feeling, when you suddenly see what it is about, that is when you take off, that's when you can begin to act it. It is the audience, after all, who should be feeling as well, if not more than, the actor.

MAROWITZ:

It's that second stage that I would like to define, if I can, because I think every performer can understand what it's like to experience emotion either in rehearsal or in performance, but this second stage that you are describing, which is in a sense the sculpting or formulation of that emotion into means that affect the audience, what does *that* actually consist of? Is it something that you rely on your technique to do? What is that second stage?

JACKSON:

At its best, when it works really well, when that energy goes from the stage into the auditorium and is returned, it is dependent upon the audience. It is not always the actor's fault that great nights in the theatre are so few and far between. I think from an acting point of view, it has to do with concentration. It is imposing the reality of your world in such a concentrated way that you suck them into you. Then, when they are sucked into you, they reinforce everything you do. There isn't really a "method" that I could be lucid about that produces that, other than being prepared for it to happen if it's going to happen. And the only way to be prepared for it to happen if it's going to happen is to have done all the work that is humanly possible for you to do—not only on your own but with the rest of the people you are acting with.

MAROWITZ:

As you perform on the stage, are you aware of audience reaction per se; that is, beyond the obvious reactions of laughter and applause? Are you aware of what is going on in the collective consciousness of the audience?

JACKSON:

Absolutely. That is the most potent, positive thing that you have over and above the coughing and the rustling, the eating of sweets, the shifting of bums on seats; that is what makes it a good or a bad night.

MAROWITZ:

How can you verify that your objective response of what an audience is experiencing is true? You can hear laughter; you can sometimes hear tears; you can hear applause.

JACKSON:

It has to do with the silence; it has to do with the concentration. You know what an audience is feeling by the quality of the silence—far more than by the quality of the laughter.

MAROWITZ:

> Have you ever been in a situation where the audience has sat spellbound, and at the end of the performance you became aware that, in fact, you had lost them; that they were not with you after all?

JACKSON:

> No.

MAROWITZ:

> Never?

JACKSON:

> I have never ever been surprised in that way, no. Of course, you know very early on in a performance when they're in that sort of apathetic state, and whether or not you're going to be able, in a sense, to bring them around. Those are always interesting evenings, because you have to be so much on your toes. But it's not the same kind of excitement as when you go out there and you know you have them absolutely; I mean, when they are afraid to draw breath.

MAROWITZ:

> So you really believe that silent communication between a performer and her public is verifiable?

JACKSON:

> Oh, indeed. It is most marked here in America, because Americans are a high-energy people, and they always have to demonstrate what they are feeling. Sometimes, of course, they are less than honest about that. There have been a couple of nights here where we have been doing *Strange Interlude* when they have been a bloody awful audience; I mean the play has not exerted upon them the kind of spell that it can. And yet, at the end, they stood up on their feet and cheered. And I have stood taking my curtain, saying: "Bullshit, what a load of crap artists. This is a lie. You didn't feel any of that. Nothing that you felt warrants this kind of response." And on other nights, when they haven't been able to draw breath, when there's been that real exchange of communication, it may be that the response is less vociferous, but it's much more genuine.

MAROWITZ:

Do you think that theory in any way helps the actor? Have you known dumb great actors? I mean by that, actors without intellect who were capable of great acting?

JACKSON:

When you say "known"—perhaps not known intimately, but certainly, yes.

MAROWITZ:

Would you say, generally speaking, that acting theory is not a prime requisite for the actor? There is no need for him to immerse himself in Brecht or Stanislavsky or Artaud?

JACKSON:

I can only go back to what I said earlier. If it's necessary for individual actors, then it's necessary for them. But there is no rule of thumb. The only rules of thumb that are absolute for actors, it seems to me, are the technical ones that have to do with the arena in which you work. There is no good doing anything, feeling anything, saying anything, if it can't be heard, seen, and felt by the audience.

MAROWITZ:

Would you say the technical requirements of the performance are greater than the theoretical ones?

JACKSON:

Well, they are the absolutes. I mean *the* absolute is, of course, the text of the play. If a great deal of theory helps you tackle those particular absolutes and lick them, then fine. But if you use it to avoid those absolutes, or they fail to connect up with theory, then you are up a gum tree without a paddle, so to speak.

MAROWITZ:

The cliché about acting is that its two basic requisites are concentration and relaxation. Do you believe this?

JACKSON:

I am a firm believer in concentration. Concentration brings with it a great many pluses. I don't believe in relaxation. I don't think that acting is a comfortable process, nor that the work is necessarily good if you're all enjoying it. My experience has always been that if you enjoy it, it's usually bloody awful. And I believe that stress and that kind of heightened consciousness that comes with it is very valuable. What one ideally would like is what one sees most clearly in Oriental martial arts, which is the ability to release all one's energy in a gesture and stop it with the same energy. So you constantly have that great force released and, at the same time, controlled.

MAROWITZ:

So you are never free of creative tension when you are acting?

JACKSON:

You shouldn't be. If you are without that creative tension . . . and it does happen; it's happened to me on the stage. I suddenly come out of that world and think: "What the hell am I doing? I am standing up here on this wooden platform, this make-up on my face, talking to a bunch of people who I don't know, who are sitting in the dark; I must be mad!" Then you have lost that creative tension, and the walls of disbelief have come tumbling down.

MAROWITZ:

Have you ever experienced stage fright, per se?

JACKSON:

I have stage fright every performance. It is something that gets worse the more you work. And it is obviously not only my experience, because I did a play with a most wonderful actress, a woman called Mona Washbourne, and she was then seventy-four and had been acting since she was twenty, and her fear was exactly the same as mine—and just as bad.

MAROWITZ:

One would think the more one does it, the more it would. . . .

JACKSON:

Indeed one would, but then the more one does it, the more you realize that you don't actually know *how* to do it. And to do it badly is painfully easy. And to do it well is astonishingly hard.

MAROWITZ:

Is the tension related to the ability to succeed in what you are doing? Does the tension have to do with how well or how badly you are going to deliver the goods on a particular night? Is that its origin?

JACKSON:

In a way it is. But when you say "deliver the goods," the "goods" you're trying to deliver are really somebody else's work. You are actually trying to do a play. It's not just you entertaining a group of people. That's not what one is talking about. You are actually trying to take somebody else's work and change what is happening to those people out there. And that is very difficult.

MAROWITZ:

Is that really what's in your mind? Are you really concerned about changing the attitudes of your audience?

JACKSON:

I don't know that I'm concerned about changing their attitudes in a permanent way. What I am concerned with is that something happens to them; that that two hours, four hours, five hours, or whatever time spent in the theatre, is entirely specific; that it will never be like that again for them. That is really what one is working for—that something happens.

MAROWITZ:

So you are not directly concerned with the social, political, or philosophical attitudes of your audience?

JACKSON:

It would be nice if I lived in a society where a political or social ideology went hand in glove with what happens on the stage. I saw Eckerhard Schall of the Berliner Ensemble when he came to Riverside Studios to do his one-man show of Brecht poems and songs. There was one of the greatest actors I have ever seen in my life. It is clear that part of the quality of his work stems from the reality of his living in a society where what he does is regarded highly—not only on its own level as theatre, but where it is used as a tool to create the kind of society that those people want. That is a dimension that one would never see either in my country or in America. But over and above that, essentially what one wants in every performance is that *something happens*.

MAROWITZ:

Is there a usefulness to the artist in drama criticism?

JACKSON:

Absolutely none.

MAROWITZ:

Haven't you found over the years that drama criticism has provided an insight into what you have done on the stage, given you something you've been able to use constructively?

JACKSON:

Never ever, no.

MAROWITZ:

Well, no point in pursuing that one. Tell me this: Is there a vestige of sexism in the actor/director relationship? Does the fact that most directors are men affect that relationship in any way?

JACKSON:

Directors will pursue arguments with actresses where they back off from actors. They will attempt to impose their opinion more on an actress than they would dare to do with an actor. And certain directors will treat actresses as though they are, by virtue of being female, essentially hysterical and need to be cajoled, flattered, and manipulated into a performance.

MAROWITZ:

The reason I asked this is because over the past few years, some women have come to resent the fact that in a rehearsal situation, they often find themselves under the thumb, as it were, of a male who happens to be the director of the play. Whereas once upon a time this was never a factor, it has, in recent years, become one. Consciously or unconsciously, they resent being given instructions by a man.

JACKSON:

I think those actresses are simply exercising the benefit of hindsight from the post-feminist movement. That is not what I'm talking about. If you can't take instructions from a director, then why have a director in the first place? You have to give them the benefit of the doubt. And if what they're suggesting is wrong, then you tell them it's wrong. If they refuse to accept it, then you have to go your own way. When it comes to the performance, they are not there, so you have to trust your own judgment. That's not what I was talking about. I was referring to a certain cut-off point beyond which a director will not push a male actor, because if he does, there is danger of a physical confrontation. There is an innate masculine respect for males which some directors do not have for females, so sometimes they will be less reasonable arguing with an actress than they would with an actor—not because her argument is any less valid but simply because she's a woman.

MAROWITZ:

But isn't there a reverse corollary there—namely, that very strong, authoritarian actresses often tend to intimidate men?

JACKSON:

Oh, yes, that is definitely true. But these all seem to me to be pointless discoveries, because this is a line of argument that implies the best work can only be done under the most perfect conditions. Well, that's crap. The best work has to be done where you are doing it, and no one is going to give you perfect conditions. You're never going to get the ideal mix-match of people to work with. You have to be able to work anywhere with everyone, so why worry about it? The next step along that road is that you begin to choose the members of your audience. Well, that's not going to happen, so it doesn't seem to be very important.

MAROWITZ:

Have you had experiences with individual directors from which you have drawn some very specific, significant lesson?

JACKSON:

Certainly working with Brook and you when we were doing the Theatre of Cruelty Season at the R.S.C. That was like coming across an oasis in the desert. There you were, formulating, in a very concrete, tangible form, ideas that one could work with—and through—to produce results which I had never seen in my then-experience of British theater. That experience, I suppose, is the most tangible lesson I've learned and which hopefully has informed all the work I've ever done. It made me see that the ideal is possible. That it's possible to release twelve people from the prison of their individuality without *losing* their individuality

—and actually create something which is greater than the sum of its parts.

MAROWITZ:

Are those elements at stake in what one tends to call commercial productions?

JACKSON:

Not only in commercial productions. They're at stake every time you put a group of actors together in whatever situation. I would think the star system is more rancidly in play in the R.S.C. and the National Theatre than in any commercial situation. They always say it isn't, but it is.

MAROWITZ:

Are you saying that the major subsidized companies, such as the R.S.C. and the National, are more prone to the evils of commercial theatre than the commercial theatre?

JACKSON:

Yes, without the responsibility of it, because in the commercial theatre, when you fail, you're off—out of work. But the big subsidized theatres are cushioned. They are there from year to year whether people go to those theatres or not—which can produce a quite awful situation.

MAROWITZ:

Finally, what advice would you give to a young actress who is just starting on her first professional engagement?

JACKSON:

The one lesson that I learned from drama school—I don't know if this is of any value to anybody, but it's been of value to me—is: You are your own instrument, and you are as good as that instrument is. Nobody else does it for you, actually. If you can't respond and express, then there's no good in "feeling" anything.

MAROWITZ:

And how do you keep your instrument in the best shape?

JACKSON:

I'm fortunate. For me, it seems to be work. I think plays are great gymnasiums. They lick you into shape quicker than anything.

MAROWITZ:

You don't subscribe, then, to that old, romantic view that the actress has to have a variety of life experiences in order to be resourceful enough to tackle all the great roles?

JACKSON:

No, I don't. There is, obviously, the accident of simply time being lived which is valuable, but I think imagination is a far more valuable tool than actual experience.

MAROWITZ:

Is it something like a furnace that you can constantly stoke?

JACKSON:

Yes, and hopefully when you're actually working on a play, there are people who can fire your imagination and stoke it for you. I am much more interested in the input that comes from imagination than from direct experience, because direct experience always seems to be a limitation. With direct experience, you are actually trying to reproduce an image that is clear; that actually *was*. I think when you shatter that image and make it into something else, then something really interesting happens.

12

Flotsam and Jetsam

The rehearsal process is the quintessential encounter group, in which a number of different temperaments coalesce or collide in the service of a work of art that is as hungry for disentanglement and self-awareness as any neurotic or depressive who ever rallied to the call of Gestalt.

There once was an actor who prided himself on the fact that his performance never altered one iota from one day to the next. "You will find," he told his director proudly, "that my hundredth performance is exactly like the one I gave on opening night."

The director came to see it and found that the actor was telling the truth. The next day he sacked him.

"But for months now I've done the role exactly as we rehearsed it," the actor protested. "Except for one thing," the director said, "I rehearsed it to develop."

A big and bellowing row is the surest way to create a new burst of concentration among a company of actors. The public release of tension acts like a purgative clearing the air and encourages a vigorous return to work. Of course, an endless series of rows, like an endless series of purgatives, only weakens the system and can produce nervous exhaustion and physical debilitation. But often, one good tirade is worth a dozen pep talks.

During a particularly trying rehearsal in which an actress could not achieve the emotional climax required by the scene, she asked to be excused. The director refused and instructed her to try the scene again, but it was no better than before. After repeating the moment eight or nine times, always to no avail, the actress broke down into hysterical tears, tossing furniture off the stage and grazing her forehead on the table. "Can I go home now?" she asked wearily, rubbing her bruised head and sobbing. "What?" said the director incredulously. "And waste all that warm-up?!"

The way in which a director responds to an actor's suggestion that is superior to his own sets the tone for the entire rehearsal period.

The actor who could not assimilate his director's ideas suggested alternatives of his own, which, in effect, reversed the instructions he was being given. After several more attempts to do it the director's way, he protested: "I just don't feel comfortable with it!"

"Neither did Michelangelo on his back under the ceiling of the Sistine Chapel, but he didn't ask the building to be turned topsy-turvy."

Whenever a play gets into trouble, three clichés immediately spring to life: pace, energy, and thrust. They are all euphemisms for "better."

Of all these words, *energy* is the most deceptive, for in acting, as in sports, the value of increased energy is that it sharpens skill. If it does not, if it is just an increase of energy per se and does not fill up the interstices of a role, it is nothing more than unharnessed physical effort and is bound to be counterproductive.

A role is an amalgam of energy units, each of which requires the translation of energy into intention, attitude, and meaning. Calling for more energy without deciding how this energy is to be used is like building a supercharged sports car and neglecting to fit a steering wheel.

Sometimes energy burns most effectively in quiet, still, and "un-energetic" moments. Energy that is visible *as* energy in its own right, is merely fuel not yet converted into power.

Once there was an actor who prided himself on his ability to find new and different angles on his character day after day. No sooner had he hatched one new idea than he began to initiate another. Not a day passed that he didn't invent and incorporate some new "find" in his role. After the play had been playing one week, he found to his surprise that he had been sacked, and so confronted the director to know the reason why.

"A butterfly is more colorful than a spider," answered the director, "but it leaves no web behind."

Sometimes a bad director is a good company's greatest blessing. It is the collective realization of his perilous inadequacy that encourages actors, out of a sense of self-preservation, to summon up their most creative energies.

An actor refused to wear the costume provided by the designer of the production, insisting it was "wrong" for his character. "But it's exactly like the drawing we showed you on the first day of rehearsal, and then you thought it was marvelous."

"That man died three and a half weeks ago," the actor replied.

No matter how contentedly the actor has lived in the director's house throughout rehearsals, the director's departure is the actor's cue to redecorate extensively.

A playwright who was sitting in on the rehearsals of his play became aware of a telling pause in the middle of what he took to be one of his best lines. He approached the director, who appeared to be letting it pass, and complained: "That pause was never there when I first wrote the play."

"No," replied the director, "neither was the actor."

The buzz of a theatre audience before the curtain rises is a sure indication of how a performance will go. Absence of preperformance chatter almost always spells disaster. A good solid hum in the house is a harbinger of positive audience reaction.

There is a certain litany that is always intoned when a comedy is going badly. With endless variations, it consists of:

"They're too self-conscious to react out loud."

"They're laughing quietly to themselves."

"They're enjoying it in their own way."

In most cases, these are euphemistic engravings on tombstones, dogged refusals to accept the fact that the loved one is dead.

Even more remarkable than these self-deceptions are the hallucinations experienced by actors during a bad performance whereby a fugitive titter is transformed into an uproarious cachinnation, or a cough into a vocal proclamation of assent. I have heard actors construe a nose-blow into a burst of approval or a collective rustle of programs into a flurry of applause. In a theatre in Birmingham, at the curtain call of a particularly dismal British drama at which a member of the audience called out "Give over!" (which roughly translated means "Please desist from any further activity"), the lead actor assured me that someone had cried out "Bravo!" Almost any sound an audience makes is capable of being metamorphosed by desperate actors into a sign of affirmation. The actor, the undisputed master of illusion, is just as frequently the victim of delusion as well.

An actress was opposed to a director's piece of business. After perfunctorily trying it and dismissing it, she said:. "I'm sorry—that just doesn't work for me."

"Perhaps you're not paying it enough," said the director, instructing her to try it again.

A director returning to a play after it has opened and launched its run is like a man trying to revive a love affair with a mistress who has since married and had twelve children.

An actor who had not done his homework and therefore blew his lines from one moment to the next, railed and abused himself in front of the entire company. No sooner did he jumble his text or drop his cue than he would start swearing and berating himself for his ineptitude and stupidity. After several minutes of this behavior, the director stopped the rehearsal and said: "If anyone castigated me as fiercely as you are castigating yourself, I would quit. On the other hand, if anyone deserved the abuse you are heaping on yourself, he should, by all rights, be fired."

The actor, after a moment, requested permission to rehearse with script in hand, and the remainder of the day passed very quietly.

"Why," said the director to the intransigent actor, "why can't you play this role the way you did on the first reading?"

"For the same reason the chicken cannot get back into the egg," answered the actor.

Extreme fatigue is often the most fertile period for inspiration—almost as if all apparent routes must first be exhausted before that secret, winding trail that leads to the high ground can be detected.

A writer whose play had already been pared down to the bone was implored by a director to "cut ten minutes more from the first act." The writer agreed to think about it overnight. When he returned the next day, the director asked him if he had decided what was to be cut. "Yes," said the writer, "take three minutes out of the pauses of the two leading players, three minutes out of the bridge music, and four minutes from the intermission."

A jovial rehearsal period, although socially pleasing, burns away the grit that is inseparable from creative work. Acting may be a labor of love, but when it is more love than labor, it falls into that trap of self-indulgence that is constantly sprung for it.

"It doesn't work," says the actor.
"I thought it *was* working," says the actress.
"How can we make it work?" asks the cast.
"Do you remember that bit that wasn't working?" says the author. "Well, I thought of a way to make it work."
"*Now* it's working," says the director.
"All that work," says the critic, "for something that could never in a million years work."

After reluctantly rehearsing a group curtain call, an old, very experienced actor accustomed to taking a call on his own approached the director and explained that his numerous years of experience, his status, and his reputation entitled him to a solo call. The director listened attentively and agreed. "Tomorrow night," he said, "the problem will be remedied."
At the end of the performance, he instructed the entire cast—except for this actor—not to appear at the curtain call. When the curtain rose, the experienced actor took the call on his own. When the curtain rose again, he was still standing there and received another

round of applause. By the time he had had his fourth call and none of the members of the cast had appeared, the audience began to boo and catcall. He pleaded with the director, who was in the wings, to send out the rest of the actors and ring down the curtain. The director refused. The solo curtain call continued, and the din of the audience's disapproval was deafening.

The really brilliant director is the man who can confront his cast after his production has been roasted in the press and convey the impression that he is unchanged.

During rehearsals of a new and difficult play, the lead actor, a man of considerable reputation, complained regularly to the director that he had a problem with the character. The director, who was delighted to have obtained the services of such an illustrious performer, pooh-poohed his objections and assured him that from "out front," there was no problem at all, and that he should just continue doing precisely what he *was* doing.

When the play opened, the reviews were uniformly bad and the audience reaction overwhelmingly negative. Everyone agreed that the lead actor had been miscast. When the director saw him again, he took him to one side and said: "Why didn't you come to me if you had a problem?"

At the end of a good performance, the actor relinquishes the visage of his character, revealing the face of the person underneath. If he does not, if the face of the man who takes the curtain call is the same as the man who performed the role, something is lacking either in the actor or in the character. In order to confirm the existence of a true performance, a curtain call should present the actor divested of every stitch of artistic camouflage, as it were, naked to the world.

An actor appearing in a serious play with light moments believed he was succeeding only if the audience crowned his efforts with laughter. As a result of this notion, he created innumerable comic moments in his performance. When the director pointed out that he was ruining the mood of the piece with gratuitous bits of comic invention, the actor said: "Can't you hear them? I'm getting all of my laughs," confident that that settled the matter.

The next evening, during the end of one of his most dramatic scenes, the actor was horrified to hear a member of the audience cackling with laughter. Try as he could to wring pathos out of the moment that had always worked before, this isolated laughter nullified all his efforts. Towards the end of the scene, he began to recognize the voice of the helplessly amused patron. It was the director.

"You ruined my performance," the actor fumed at him backstage. "Ruined it?" answered the director incredulously, "I was only giving you a few more laughs."

The most common noise in a theatre is the sound of a misguided actor barking up the wrong tree.

There has never been a production, no matter how enthusiastically begun, that I did not feel like cancelling in the middle.

During a trying rehearsal period in which a director changed his mind time and time again, the actor suddenly threw down his script and protested: "One day you tell me to do it this way, the next day, another. It's never been the same two days running. Don't you know your own mind?"

"Perfectly," answered the director, "but I don't yet know the playwright's."

A character man of about sixty-eight was cast to play an old retainer, a role to which he was perfectly suited, but once rehearsals began, he proceeded to give the character a painfully slow gait and the crumpled posture of a man twice his age. He so exaggerated the age of the character that it became unbearable to watch.

The director took him aside and said he had had a brainstorm in regard to the character. Instead of making him an old retainer, he was going to play him as a *young* retainer—a man of about thirty or forty years old. The old character man was delighted with the new twist. He dropped his shuffling gait and senile mannerisms. After the opening, he was highly complimented for his performance, and one critic wrote that it was so refreshing to see an aged character played with such charm and lightness. The character man, reading that and believing he had failed totally in the part, approached the director and offered to give up his role. "Nonsense," said the director. "I realized in the middle of rehearsals that my idea about a young retainer was ridiculous, and when I saw you gradually abandon the idea, I heaved a sigh of relief. Now it's turned out splendidly." The older character man was confused, but withdrew his notice.

Towards the end of the highly successful run, he could be heard bad-mouthing the director: "Would you believe it, he actually wanted me to play this character as if he were thirty or forty years old. Thank God there are still some old pros in this business, or these 'young geniuses' would ruin everything!"

Uncontrollable giggling at rehearsals is a sign of sanity and, although not to be encouraged, should be tolerated—if for no other reason than to affirm the absurdity of grown men and women carrying on like children. Anyone who cannot see the ludicrousness of what actors and actresses do for a living is too irretrievably humorless to be in the theatre.

Theatrical collage (as in *The Marowitz Hamlet*, *A Macbeth*, *An Othello*, etc.) combines speed, discontinuity, and dramatic juxtaposition. Speed enables it to deliver a maximum amount of information in a minimum amount of time. Discontinuity permits it to express interior meanings that in more conventional structures are revealed through the more plodding movements of unfolding psychology. Dramatic juxtapositions enable it to convey contrast and contradiction in such a way as to provide more dramatic information than is possible through sequential development. The effect of this swift, fragmentary method is to generate a surreal style that communicates experience from a subjective standpoint, thereby shifting the focus of events from an anterior to an interior reality.

Although in form and approach collage eschews psychological realism, within the confines of each of its brief segments, the laws of verifiable human conduct apply. Like a painter's collage whose overall effect is odd and disorienting, each individual piece is made up of recognizable elements that, extracted from its context, appear as real objects in a known world. It is this fusion of disparate, realistic content in the midst of surreal form that poses the greatest problem for actors, as it enjoins them to express moments of true feeling while tied to the wheel of swiftly changing rhythms and to be as faithful to the truth of those moments as they are to the tempi that drive them from one to the other.

Discontinuity, if it is only an arbitrary division of Aristotelian time, is nothing more than a gratuitous stylistic device. A film, for example, that wilfully uses flashbacks and flash-forwards to convey what is essentially a progressive storyline is not really a departure from conventional narrative form. It is only when the accumulations of dramatic strands do *not* make up the sum total of their parts that we have successfully escaped the stranglehold of narrative. However, if that succeeds only in producing obscurity, it is no boon. The dramatic value of discontinuity, particularly in the case of classics, is that it provides a useful by-product of the continuous narrative from which it has been derived. An effective way of retelling a story whose main strands are generally known is to skim its surface, reangle its moving parts, and abstract it just enough to provide a new and unexpected vantage point on the original.

We have thus far only scratched the surface of theatrical collage. Like so many innovations associated with the period of its inception, it is today considered merely a "sixties phenomenon," vaguely associated with the cut-ups of William Burroughs and the "randomness" experiments of John Cage. But just as Dada resurfaced as surrealism and later as Happenings and Performance Art, collage, as a viable dramatic form will revive in thirty or forty years and be jubilantly "rediscovered."

Since the most salient characteristics of late-twentieth-century experience are fragmentation and the mixture of antithetical styles, it seems to me inevitable that theatrical collage will, in a matter of decades, oust Aristotelian structure once and for all. In fifty years, no playwright will contemplate "developing" a theme through sequential narrative. Rather, he will coalesce contrasting pieces that imply narrative development and concern himself mainly with the optimum dramatic effect to be had from the juxtaposition of its many parts.

Although such "parts" will still—ultimately—constitute a "sum total," it will occur to no one to "add them up" in order to arrive at that total. That much-touted "bottom line" will be eradicated from theatrical process, and each dramatic numeral will have acquired its own particular significance. As a result of this linear (antinuclear) structure, the final act of theatrical performance will be the audience's and not the artist's. How the public orders the performance in its mind and through its feelings—artists' prerogatives notwithstanding—will determine what it is really about.

But then, is that so very different from what happens today?

There is no loneliness more inconsolable than the director's on an opening night.

An actor who found it difficult to understand elementary terms once asked a director to define the word *motivation*. The director, who had grown tired of manufacturing reasons for the actor, replied: "Motivation is a fairytale a director invents to persuade an actor to do as he wishes. For instance, if I told you Santa would arrive as soon as you fell asleep, you'd immediately go to bed."

An actor who felt his character was suddenly motivated to rise, stride across the stage, and vehemently slam the door, did precisely that. The director, who felt this behavior was much too extreme for that kind of character, said nothing.

The following week, he suggested the actor need not slam the door but only rise and cross towards it. The actor did so. The week after that, he wondered whether the actor had to cross at all—whether the rise was perhaps a strong enough move on its own. After a few attempts, the cross was removed. In the third week, the actor found it more and more difficult to rise at just that moment. During the previews, he remained seated and only turned his head in the direction of the door. On opening night, he didn't even move his head, but only darted his eyes towards the door. The director was very pleased and told him so.

"You're a rotten bastard," said the actor to the director, who assumed the remark was intended good-naturedly.

"The basis of all comedy is truth." That is one of the most treasured of all theatrical clichés, and, although there is a kernel of truth in the maxim, it means almost nothing without assiduous qualification.

Comedy comes in many different shapes and sizes. Some comedy is based upon accurate observation of human behavior, but in broad farce, for example, comedy derives from an exaggeration of truthful behavior that is tantamount to a distortion of the truth. In such cases, to simulate the "truthful behavior" of a cuckolded husband or a faithless wife would produce not comedy but pathos. (In Roger Planchon's production of *George Dandin*, for example, the director ironed out all the comic implications of the play, and instead of domestic comedy produced a grim essay on marital infidelity.) In the case of broad farce, the degree and size of exaggeration are the essential comic factors. What the actors do is highly tangential to commonly observed "truthful behavior."

In satirical comedy, where characters are made to reveal traits, attitudes, and qualities that they might ordinarily conceal, the "truth" depends on not verisimilitude but inflation. Of course, there is a connection between what is being extended and the "real" qualities on which it is based, but because the performance delivers an insight rather than a surface reflection of people and events, the determining factor is not "reality" but its imaginative extension.

The reason the homily about comedy being based on truthful behavior is so dangerous is that people tend to take it literally, without appreciating the fact that the key phrase is "based on." When a performer "bases" a performance on something outside of himself, he is incorporating all the artifice and falsifications that make art different from life. In one sense, no artist can possibly create anything which isn't, in some way or other, a version of observed social and psychological reality. A common humanity is what all of us have in common. The point at which meaningful distinctions occur is precisely the moment we begin to embellish, underscore, inflect, or transform that "truth" for the purposes of revealing it artistically, and when we begin to do that, the departure from truth has already begun.

The known universe is the basis for all scientific invention, but discoveries arise only when these known ingredients are rethought and compounded differently. So in the theatre, it is the inversion and reversion of the truth that are at a premium—not the unadorned truth itself.

Bad directors tend to come in two general types—Kerenskyites, weak-willed democrats who can easily be usurped, and Trotskyites, doctrinal intellectuals who talk a good show but can never get it together. The best directors are almost always Stalinists.

Nothing is but interpretation makes it so.

An actor's losing his lines after he has got a new idea about his role is a healthy sign. It means some burgeoning impulse is breaking up a structure that has solidified too early.

Because of ego and lack of objectivity, it is very difficult for the actor to distinguish between useless criticism and a review that pinpoints a telling flaw in his performance. Most criticism is like the braying of asses, although occasionally the sound of a lark breaks through.

The first performance before an audience is like a powerful searchlight trained onto a work that hitherto existed only in half-light. After it, the director has two clear choices: either he acts upon his new insights, or he tramples them down in favor of his original conception. The second course involves much less rehearsal time.

I rethink, therefore I am.

Through men such as Copernicus, Kepler, and Galileo, we discovered that we were not the center of the universe but only a small particle of an incalculable vastness. Through Darwin, we gradually came to accept that we were in no way special in creation but merely a descendant from the animal kingdom whose instincts and heredity still conditioned our lives. Freud, by demonstrating that despite our struttings and our strivings, we were the helpless victims of our unconscious, destroyed our last vestige of independence.

Freud has been the "last word" in theatrical theory, and even Artaud, whose ideas have had such recent prominence, has merely reshuffled the dream-vs.-reality clichés of the surrealists, who were themselves the artistic progeny of the psychoanalysts. All of modern psychology, from Freud through Adler, Reich, Maslow, and Laing, infers an undetected human complexity of which psychology is only the exhalation.

Behind the text is the psychological subtext, but behind that is a labyrinth in which myths and legends about our species swill about undetected. If psychological truth were the be-all and the end-all, our drama would need comprise only case histories, but because our reality is compounded of fantasies other than daydreams, traumas, and complexes, we have to dig deeper than first-stage motivations.

The Method enables us to see a little way beyond the surface, but we know from the complexity of our inner lives that beyond psychology lies a highly personal maze in which history, sociology, anthropology, and metaphysics intersect. If we acknowledge the richness and mystery of what exists beyond the surface of things, we must also acknowledge the need to express those intimations in our art. Settling for less is a form of falsification. Being overimpressed by verisimilitude is a convenient way of halting our inquiries into those deeper and less tractable areas.

Artaud's great virtue is that he urged us to recognize a variety of inner experience that, if we are to be proper artists, must be dealt with in some concrete form. The onus is on the actor. It is up to him to find means of expressing the inexpressible and to acknowledge that merely by refining his arts of imitation and representation, he is flogging a dead horse. The sooner he can "identify" with what is now unidentifiable in his nature—the substance of his illusions and his fantasies, the hieroglyphics of those interior dialogues that are constantly going on both in sleep and in wakefulness—the sooner art will reveal the meaning of that interior world on which our outer world is predicated

But the contemporary actor is not even searching out these areas. His disciplines are restricted to voice, movement, and the repetition of material that monotonously reiterates the homilies of (so-called) psychological-realistic truth. Theatre in almost every country and on almost every stage tends to be the assembly of recognizable external behavior to the accompaniment of familiar speech. We praise a play if it "dramatizes" some scorching truth, that is, tells us again—effectively and with a maximum of conflict and suspense—what we already know. But when will it tell us what we do *not* know? Only, in my view, when it succeeds in creating a diction of ideas and emotions that is not yet apparent but that, nevertheless, is common to our everyday experience.

There are a handful of playwrights one might cite as touching the border of this "other theatre" (Beckett, Ionesco, Genet, Bernhardt, Handke, Straus) but the overriding fact is that it does not exist in the work of writers, nor can it. It is a relationship between experience and expression that has not yet been developed and that, if it ever does come about, will be the product of the actor's imagination working actively and spatially in some new stylistic context yet to be defined. All one can say conclusively about it is that it will not be harnessed to language as we know it. It will not "tell" us anything. It will be a theatre not of fiery speeches but of burning bushes.

13

Brave New World

The year is 2986.

A new play is to be performed.

The Mediator has met with the playwright, taken his first draft, revised it according to his own lights, and created a rough mise-en-scène that has thoroughly subsumed the writer's work. Having divided the piece into a series of scenic units and audio-visual components, he proceeds to select the actors.

Rather than call the company to a first reading, he sends a copy of the material to all members of the cast. When rehearsals begin, each comes in turn to the theatre, and the Mediator works with him individually. He delves into the background of the actor's character, discusses the intentions of various scenes, and tries to conjure up an image of the physical and psychic nature of the character the actor is to portray. He then puts him through a variety of improvised situations—some of which bear upon the material of the play, and others of which have nothing directly to do with the play. He encourages the actor to imagine moods, states, and circumstances in which his character might find himself. He conjures up fictitious people and imaginary situations the character might have encountered. None of these impinge directly on the material of the role. That done, he tells the actor to go away and memorize his lines.

With each character, the same process is repeated. Each actor has four or five weeks of preliminary work with the Mediator and is then sent off to learn his role. The actors never encounter one another. Each one works privately with the Mediator, then goes away to cogitate his findings.

After a while, characters who interact with each other in the play are summoned to rehearsals together. The actual text of the play is never dealt with. Instead, the actors begin to bounce off one another in invented situations. They improvise scenes, incidents, fantasies, improbabilities, none of which occur in the play but all of which are conceivable in relation to it. These scenes are suggested first by the Mediator and then by the actors themselves.

They are structured loosely according to the actor's suggestions and then performed in front of the Mediator, who appraises them as an audience of one. The actors then assess the Mediator's reactions, deciding whether or not they agree with them. No one attempts to reach any final judgment about the scenes. If the Mediator disapproves of what the actors have done, he merely posits his adverse opinion. If the actors disagree with the Mediator their reactions stand on a par with his. The exchange is free and open. There is never any question of who is "right" or "wrong." It is never assumed that the actors are there to "take direction." The exploration of possibilities among all members of the cast continues for four or five weeks, always improvised; at no time do they rehearse the text that the actors have already learned.

At about this time, the company begins to discuss the thematic implications of the work, its sociopolitical and philosophical constituents—what the play means; what it is about; whether it is moral or immoral, decent or indecent (always assuming it can legitimately be one or the other), and what attitudes it should engender in the minds of an audience.

Through rigorous examination of the nature of artistic organization, the company will learn to recognize the appearance of a dominant personality in their midst attempting to impose his will upon others—surreptitiously restoring the insidious influence of the archaic director. At the first trace of such egotistical intrusion, they will pounce upon the upstart, pluck out the best of his ideas, add them to the collective whole, and then reintegrate his personality into the ensemble from which it transgressed. The principle of an overriding collective intelligence will be so devoutly observed, and the sin of unbridled individualism so severely castigated, that no one will dare to break away from the selfless interconnectiveness of the ensemble effort. The virtues of individuality (upon which all acting is predicated) will be subsumed by the cooperative effort of the company, but its power to usurp the general consensus will be resolutely quashed. By these means, the firmament of the ensemble will become the inevitable framework for the appearance of "stars" (i.e., outstandingly creative individuals).

In the final stage of rehearsals, the actors come to the theatre to view the work of the designers. They begin to inhabit the stage settings, testing out the new habitations. Simultaneously, they bring to the costume designer the clothes they themselves have designed, purchased, or borrowed. The costume designer promptly adjusts his preconceived notions of the actors' idea of character attire. The principle that actors are responsible for the selection of their clothes is unquestioningly accepted by the costume designer. He, like the Mediator before him, is there to comment and opine from his own specialist's viewpoint. The final choice is the actor's. Everyone, including the costume designer, understands that. Once their discussion is over, the costume designer leaves, never to return.

Likewise, the actors respond to the work of the set designer, either approving or amending his ideas. If they feel a piece of furniture is the wrong color or the wrong shape, the set designer alters it to accommodate the actors. If the basic decor is not what certain members of the cast expected, he knows he will be obliged to alter his conception. If there is strong disagreement between the actors, the Mediator will be called in to monitor these discussions, and when they are done, he will convey to the set designer the prevailing view of the actors. He may have input of his own during these discussions, but it is understood that the actors make the final determination, and he is there simply to facilitate their preferences.

The lighting designer will demonstrate the plot he has worked out for the play. The actors, shuttling between the auditorium and the stage, will gauge the efficiency of these choices and either approve or alter them. Again, the Mediator will be there to mediate between the actor and the designer if a dispute arises, but the actor's prerogatives will always determine the final result.

Now that the basic production choices have been made and the actors have acclimatized themselves to the setting, explored the background of their roles with the Mediator, and discussed the thematic implications of the play, the performance is ready to commence. Without the preliminaries of runthroughs, dress rehearsals, or previews, the audience will be invited to the opening week (as opposed to the opening night, an archaic convention that will have been dispensed with half a century before). Each performance will be a combustion of all the ingredients painstakingly prepared. It will be understood that there is no compunction for each performance to be exactly the same. Since the physical components are constant, it is accepted that the inner chemistry may range freely within the parameters of character already decided upon by each individual actor. The rhythms of each performance will certainly change from night to night, and the staging, never having been imposed by a director, will have variation built into its geography.

As the play progresses and certain doubts arise on the part of one character or another, actors will have the freedom to alter the shape and thrust of their role, changing text as they see fit. As they discover new aspects as a result of altered performance experience, it is taken for granted that that will change the way in which their roles are interpreted from night to night. If an individual actor's conception of his role changes radically from what was originally conceived, the other actors in the company will be obliged to find ways and means to adapt to these changes (since they too have the freedom to alter *their* roles according to the insights they gain from their own performance).

Throughout, the Mediator who has never "staged" or "interpreted" the roles for his company, will observe the changes in the performance and, at given intervals, provide objective and informed reaction to the actor's work. Proceeding from his comments, the actors may decide to change their choices or mode of delivery, but they recognize that they are not obliged to do so—just as the Mediator recognizes that he has no right to impose his views upon them. Throughout, he will be a sympathetic "third party," feeding input to the actors, designers, and technicians; giving them the benefit of his changing perceptions. After a while, he will realize, as does the entire company, that he too has lost his objectivity, and so he will be retired (along with the author and designers, who departed earlier), and another, especially informed "sympathetic onlooker" will be brought in to take his place.

When the company is satisfied that the play has assumed its essential shape, the critics will be invited to the performance. This viewing may be two or three months after the play's public opening, a date collectively determined by the company. On the evening of the day their notices appear, the critics will be obliged to attend a public forum in the theatre, where they will be expected to justify their reactions before a panel composed of actors, Mediator, designer, playwright, and the general public.

If, during the course of the forum, they are unable to justify their judgments, naturally they will retract or modify them in the next day's paper. Should they be guilty of consistent misjudgment, the theatre will have the right to revoke their right to criticize, the case for such revocation of rights to be heard in a court of aesthetic law, where the panel of judges will be made up of artists, poets, journalists, editors, and enlightened members of the theatre-going public. (It is a tacit assumption that the critic's right to exist depends upon the artist's recognition of those talents and skills that qualify him for the job.)

Towards the end of the run, the playwright will be invited back to see the play refined from his raw material. He will then be invited to "write it down"—not necessarily as it exists on the stage, but in whatever form he chooses. The play may then be published by the writer, but simultaneous with this publication, a "transcriber" will publish a printed version of the performance created by the company. The two versions will be quite independent entities despite their obvious similarities. Future companies will have the option of producing the company's version or the author's, depending on their preference.

During the course of the run, to retain freshness, actors will switch roles with other actors. In this way, almost every actor in the company will be able to experience the character of another before returning to his original role. (Where desirable, males will switch with females and vice versa.) The Mediator, having absorbed the background of each character from his private study at the start of rehearsals, will function as a standing understudy, ready to take over any role that may fall vacant because of sickness or the drying up of an actor's creative enthusiasm, it being an article of faith that when an actor grows bored with his character and can no longer sustain him in performance, he is honor-bound to relinquish it.

When the actors feel they have exhausted all the possible permutations of their roles and every interpretation of which the play is capable, it will be ready for closure. The length of the run will be strictly determined by the company's assessment of the production's durability. Since they are in its midst every night, they are the best judges of its freshness or decay. When they feel the time is right, considerations of public demand notwithstanding, the production will be discontinued and the next project begun.

Since the late nineteenth century, that is, since the theories of Wagner, Appia, and Craig gained prominence, the whole thrust of theatrical production has been towards unity of effect. That has usually meant the predominance of the director, ostensibly in the service of the playwright.

The single most important development in dramaturgy during the twentieth century has been the dismissal of the Aristotelian notion of chronology and the unities. The surrealists began to subvert it in the 1920s, and Einstein, Brecht, and Artaud routed it thoroughly in the last half of the century. When the atom got split, the notion of continuity and sequential development got split along with it. In aesthetic terms, nuclear fission has meant fragmentation, discontinuity, the mixture of antithetical styles, and the invasion of mixed media into the previously exclusive confines of theatrical art. Although the well-made play lingers on even into the mid- and late twentieth century and there is an unquenchable nostalgia for the old masterworks, the aesthetics of the new century are just around the corner. A world conditioned by laser research, computer technology, and extra terrestrial exploration cannot help but alter the formulae by which art is produced.

The first victims of any new advance are always the people who held most rigidly to the obsolete ways. If that is true, the playwright will be the first to disappear in the new age of art. Because he clung to outdated theorems and could not keep up with the faster rhythms of the changing times, and because his craftsmanship has been absorbed by both actors and directors, the writer will have lost his function.

Because he is not essential to the propagation of the art form, and because his expertise is derived basically from actors and writers, the director will be the next to go.

The designers will be relegated to the positions they should have held in the first place: mere handmaidens to the actors, eunuchs at court.

The actor, sensing that his is the centrifugal power of the performing art, will take unto himself all the duties relegated to writers, directors, and designers. He will learn to transcend the endlessly spiraling mechanism of his own ego and include thematic strategy and interpretative sweep along with his ability to construct characters and essay text. His appropriation of the writer's skills will give him new and invigorating possibilities of verbal creation, and his liberation from "staging" will open up new vistas for aural and kinetic expression. (The tendency to devise his own language already exists, which is why so many playwrights have risen from the ranks of actors.) The actor will develop a new responsibility towards visual artifacts. Just as he designed the graph of his role and the shape of his speeches, he will learn to employ the arts of the sculptor, painter, builder, and environmentalist. He will recognize that he is as responsible for his setting as for his character, and once that is realized, he will determine the shape and size of the stage he deems appropriate for his performance.

Having fought and fulminated against directors for so many years, the actor will gradually acquire the skill to conceptualize the *whole* play and not merely that part of it that has been assigned to him. He will correlate themes with action, action with character, and integrate all these elements into a performance for which he will hold himself strictly accountable. He will realize that interpreting a play is only one step beyond interpreting a character *in* that play, and that if he has the intellect to devise motivation and uncover subtext, there is no reason why he cannot also marshal social and philosophic ideas into a self-generated theatrical construct.

He will remind himself that it all began with Thespis, and that when the theatre first started, the actor, the writer, and the director were three reflexes of the same creative instinct, three fingers of the same hand. He will come to recognize that for five hundred years, he has been ousted from his rightful seat of power and that writers and directors have colonized him as shamefully as the empire builders ever did the Africans or the Indians. He will learn to confront the hatred and contempt he has repressed all these centuries towards makeshift scribblers whose "gifts" consisted merely of recycling blocks of the same, monotonous old material.

He will come to recognize that despite their air of intellectual superiority, directors have, for centuries, nourished themselves on actors' ingenuity, arrogating to themselves creative ideas spawned instinctively by them. The director, he will come to see, has never been anything more than a loquacious parasite describing, after the event, sensations and effects he could never in a million years have conjured up on his own; pretending to be an intermediary between script and performance when the actor's means of expression and interpretative powers were the only media ever needed.

He will realize that a misappropriation of credit by obtuse critics over a period of two hundred years regularly attributed to directors those achievements for which actors were uniquely responsible. He will come to see that the compartmentalization of the creative process has consisted of a series of subtle plagiaries that the writer and director foisted upon the actor from the dawn of the art form—which is why, perhaps, the actor's animosity for these drones has been such a constant factor in the history of dramatic art. The unspoken hatred, the smoldering tension that ran like a current beneath all collaborations, stemmed from the fact that the actor never had the guts to confront his "fellow artists" and declare: "I can flourish without you, but without me, you cannot even begin to hypothesize an existence."

After a century filled with an endless proliferation of films, television, video, cable, laser shows, outer-space spectaculars, and an assortment of computerized audio-visual entertainment, the public will have returned to the live theatre, realizing that the eternal verities of life and death could be confronted nowhere else. A whole new breed of actors will have had to have been created, since the electronic performers, having relied exclusively on technology for their effects, will have forgotten the basic tenets of existential acting—the skills of portraying the Here and Now.

The archives will have been ransacked to rediscover the precepts of Cicero. Aristotle will have been exhumed and brought back to fashion along with the works of Shakespeare, Moliére, Ibsen, and Strindberg. Heretics will agitate for the reinstatement of Stanislavsky; small, ostracized sects championing Brecht and Artaud will have sprung up in remote crater communities or on space stations orbiting the globe.

Within a half-century, as a result of massive archaeological excavations, playhouses will have been restored. By the advent of the year 4001, with the debris of over two thousand years of media stockpiled in unpopulated underground caverns, the actor, his muscles humming like a live wire, his voice thundering with a revivified resonance, his instincts sharp as the cutting edge of a laser beam, his sensibility imploding with original perceptions and a readiness to communicate a fresh vision of the postnuclear world, will take the stage again, and a new theatrical age will dawn.

CHARLES MAROWITZ was for twelve years the artistic director of London's Open Space Theatre. He was also a close collaborator with Peter Brook at the Royal Shakespeare Company. He has directed classical and modern productions in Germany, France, Italy, Norway, Sweden, and England, where he lived for some twenty years. He now lives in California where he is associated with the Los Angeles Theatre Center.

DIRECTING
THE
ACTION

OTHER TITLES FROM THE APPLAUSE ACTING SERIES

ACTING IN FILM
(BOOK & VIDEOCASSETTE)
Michael Caine

ACTING IN RESTORATION COMEDY
(BOOK & VIDEOCASSETTE)
Simon Callow

THE END OF ACTING
Richard Hornby

MICHAEL CHEKHOV:
ON THEATER AND THE ART OF ACTING
(4 CDS & BOOKLET)
Mala Powers (ed.)

THE MONOLOGUE WORKSHOP
Jack Poggi

ON SINGING ONSTAGE
David Craig

RECYCLING SHAKESPEARE
Charles Marowitz

SHAKESCENES: SHAKESPEARE FOR TWO
John Russell Brown

SPEAK WITH DISTINCTION
Edith Skinner

STANISLAVSKI REVEALED
Sonia Moore

STANISLAVSKY TECHNIQUE: RUSSIA
Mel Gordon